Goalkeeper training methodology

Vaggelis Lappas

Goalkeeper training methodology

level 1 & 2

© 2019 Sportbook Publications
ISBN 978-618-5316-38-9

SPORTBOOK Publications
Thessaloniki, Andrea Papandreou 172, 56626, Greece
Tel: (+30) 2310.629319
http://www.sportbook.gr
e-mail: info@sportbook.gr

All rights reserved. No part of this publication may be reproduced, stored in a retrieval system, or transmitted in any form or by any means, electronic, mechanical, photocopy, recording or otherwise, without prior written permission of the copyright owner. Nor can it be circulated in any form of binding or cover other than that in which it is published and without similar condition including this condition being imposed on a subsequent purchaser.

PREFACE

The purpose of this book is not to discover anything new or innovative. Its only purpose is to put all the knowledge I have gained concerning football in order. This book was written to assist me in my daily routine when I'm working with goalkeepers, whose needs oblige me to follow this specific methodology. It helps me to analyze and customize the training routine and adapt the methodology in order to meet the needs of every goalkeeper.

My occupation with sports started in 1986 and I was lucky enough to grow up in a family where sports were very important—and with my beloved team ever since— Aetos (Eagle) Korydallou. This is where I met my first coach, Mr. Stephanos Iliadis; I'd like to thank him because even though he had no special knowledge about coaching, psychology, and so on, he trained me with his love for his occupation, always keeping in mind the fact I was first a child and then a goalkeeper. He taught me how to respect, show discipline, work and appreciate; and last but not least, he made me love the goalkeeper's position.

In 2010, I was lucky enough to meet Mr. Yiannis Samaras, who became my mentor. There's nothing I can say to express my full gratefulness for getting the opportunity to work with him. Regarding my world of football, the most beautiful things that have ever happened to me are endless hours of conversation, work, research, record keeping and analysis.

I dedicate this book to my parents, Dimitris and Maria, who educated me properly and taught me to respect everyone. I'd also like to dedicate the book to my family—Marina, Anastasia and Dimitra—who constantly offer me insatiable love, patience and support.

Finally, I'd like to thank everyone. I love you all!

CONTENTS

INTRODUCTION 9
VISION. 10
TRAINING GUIDE. 11
THE IMPORTANCE OF THE DETAILS 12
TECHNIQUE. 13
FOOTBALL COACHING TOPICS 14

CHAPTER 1: BALL FAMILIARITY 19
Drills 21

CHAPTER 2: LEARNING THE BASIC PRINCIPLES. 49
Drills 50

CHAPTER 3: HANDLING DRILLS INTRODUCTION 63
Drills 64

CHAPTER 4: SHOT STOPPING 77
Drills 78

CHAPTER 5: DIVING INTRODUCTION 91
Drills 92

CHAPTER 6: POSITIONING
Drills 102

CHAPTER 7: SAVING ON THE MOVE 111
Drills 112

CHAPTER 8: THE IMPERFECT WORLD 119
Drills 120

CHAPTER 9: ONE ON ONES 137
Drills 138

CHAPTER 10: REACTIONS 155
Drills 156

CHAPTER 11: DEALING WITH CROSSES 163
Drills 164

CHAPTER 12: DISTRIBUTION 183
Drills 184

CHAPTER 13: BACK PASSES 195
Drills 196

CHAPTER 14: PHYSICAL CONDITIONING 207
Drills 208

INTRODUCTION

Football is a team sport played with 11 players. Every team member should contribute at maximum potential in order to raise the chances of winning the game. The best teams in the world start their build-up with an exceptional goalkeeper.

Developing the skills of a goalkeeper (technically, tactically, physically, psychologically and socially) are necessary to create goalkeepers that can withstand the difficulties at the highest levels of football.

VISION

Our vision is the creation of a positive training atmosphere, where the goalkeepers will develop and evolve their techniques, and physical and psychological skills, along with creativity and understanding of the game.

If we want young goalkeepers to evolve through the process of the game, we need coaches who are not afraid to encourage, and can coach without the fear of failure. In addition, we need coaches who possess a huge variety of training methods, so they can safely guide the young goalkeepers in order to learn the game.

There is no room in our vision for overzealous adults that tend to DRILL unjustified pressure onto young players which provokes stress, or for coaches that insist on winning being the main focus. This can lead to sacrificing the learning process, the fun of the game and the personal development of the player.

Our first target concerning youth football development should be the creation of a space where the very young goalkeepers can feel the love for the position of the goalkeeper and for the game overall.

Our second target is to develop goalkeepers with excellent technique, excellent tactical understanding, extraordinary physical characteristics and skills in decision making.

The profit from this procedure is twofold:

- We enhance the chance of creating highly skilled goalkeepers with excellent technique, creativity and perception of the game.
- The positive approach and entertaining experience for the young players can secure their active role in the game for many years. They can become fans, coaches, support staff, referees or volunteers.

I cannot teach anybody anything.
I can only make them think
Socrates

TRAINING GUIDE

1. Coaches are role models for young goalkeepers. They have to be perfect in their behavior and in their appearance.
2. A coach should be approachable, pleasant and patient.
3. The working conditions depend initially from the disposition and the attitude of the coach. Facilities and training equipment come next. A good coach adapts and can always be productive.
4. The training equipment is an added help. The coaching eye and his knowledge are the basic tools for the goalkeeping coach.
5. The training duration should serve the training purpose of the module. After that, the goalkeepers should be incorporated into the team.
6. The main objective in every training module is a technically flawless execution of every drill. Without it, there can be no progress.
7. Any given correction from the coach to the goalkeepers should follow the correct technique and use questions with the positive feedback method. The corrections should be limited and precise, so they can be easily understood. You should never tell your goalkeeper what to avoid. You should always tell him what to do to in order to succeed in his objective.
8. The goalkeeper is part of the team and that means his role is active in both of its functions, defense and attack.
9. During a game, the goalkeeper touches the ball with his feet 70% of the time (this percentage is about to increase) and 30% of the time with his hands. So, a goalkeeper's training should be structured following these percentages.
10. A goalkeeper should participate in the tactical training/games with his team. That's the only way to understand the game, obtaining the much needed automatic requirements of the defensive and attacking functions of the team.
11. The know-how of modern football is necessary, thus, the goalkeeper can have a clear perception during the game, allowing him to make more accurate predictions.
12. His role is to be calm, to motivate, to encourage and to guide.

THE IMPORTANCE OF THE DETAILS

Football is a game of mistakes. The goalkeeper has to eliminate his mistakes. If he wants to succeed in that, he has to pay attention to the slightest of details and it doesn't really matter if we're talking about the training session or the game itself. The details are those that will play a definitive role in his development. That's the way he will be able to cope at maximal potential with all these difficult situations during his career. One wrong decision, slacking off for a while, a bad step or a bad hand position is more than enough to spoil a good appearance.

One can easily comprehend, that our demands from a modern coach aren't moderate. Not only should he be capable of training a goalkeeper properly, he should be continuously informed and educated about these matters. A coach must gain the trust of his players. Trust is an indispensable element for the transfer of knowledge.

A good save doesn't make you a great goalkeeper.
A mistake doesn't make you a bad goalkeeper either.

TECHNIQUE

If a goalkeeper wants to achieve high performance, he must have a perfect technique. The learning process starts from the early youth development phase, but perfection is something that a goalkeeper should always seek to achieve during his career, regardless of his level.

My opinion is that a coach should always focus on technique throughout his sessions. He should prefer reducing the number of drills and focusing on the correct execution. Improvement comes through quality and not quantity.

This learning process demands a proper methodology, patience and persistence in the detail while executing any drill. The basic concept of a training session should be progressive - 'easy to difficult' and 'simple to complicated'.

The proper training of goalkeepers depends on the proper and continuous training of goalkeeper coaches.

FOOTBALL COACHING TOPICS

Analytically, the football coaching topics are divided into 14 large categories:

1. Ball Familiarity
2. Learning the Basic Principles
3. Handling Drills Introduction
4. Shot Stopping
5. Diving Introduction
6. Positioning
7. Saving on the Move
8. The Imperfect World
9. 1 vs 1
10. Reactions
11. Dealing with Crosses
12. Distribution
13. Back Passes
14. Physical Condition

PYRAMID OF AGES

 21 years old

- Tactical topics
- Strength and conditioning training (>17 years old)

 15 years old

- Improvement and perfection of every technique
- Introduction to tactics
- Introduction to Strength & Conditioning (body weight)

 11 years old

- Learning every basic ability (movement)
- ABC's games (agility, balance, coordination, speed)
- Participating in many sports

 5 years old

PYRAMID OF TRAINING

- Physical Condition
- Back Passes
- Distribution
- Dealing with Crosses
- Reactions
- 1 vs 1
- The Imperfect World
- Saving on the Move
- Positioning
- Diving Introduction
- Shot Stopping
- Handling Drills Introduction
- Learning the Basic Principles
- Ball Familiarity

In the pyramid diagrams on the previous two pages, we see the gradation according to the proper priorities. The table below shows how we can categorize the coaching sessions according to the age of our players. I consider it to be really important that this plan is ideal. A goalkeeper's needs are unique. That means that the most important part of development is knowing what to do in every step of the methodology that we apply. That can help us evaluate better and make our training plan per week, per month, per year and per five years.

COACHING TOPIC	AGE
Ball Familiarity	5-11 years old
Learning the Basic Principles	5-11 years old
Handling Drills Introduction	8-11 years old
Shot Stopping	8-14 years old
Diving Introduction	8-14 years old
Positioning	8-14 years old
Saving on the Move	11-14 years old
The Imperfect World	14-21 years old
1 vs 1	14-21 years old
Reactions	14-21 years old
Dealing with Crosses	14-21 years old
Distribution	14-21 years old
Back Passes	14-21 years old
Physical Condition	17-21 years old

CHAPTER 1

BALL FAMILIARITY

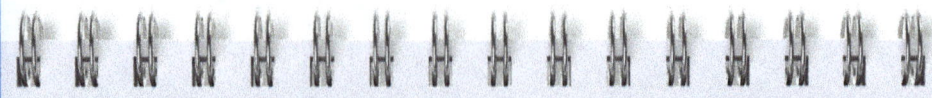

Ball Familiarity

BALL GAMES

The first thing a child needs to know when beginning to play as a goalkeeper, is the sense of being comfortable and familiar with the ball.

The first thing a child wants and needs is a ball. We must give a ball to every goalkeeper.

At the first level, there are specialized drills that can help the goalkeeper feel more comfortable with the ball. He should be trained as often as possible.

DRILL 1 — **THE BALL IN THE AIR (CHEST LEVEL) WITH STABLE LEGS (LEVEL 1)**

Objective 1 Keep the ball in the air using your hands (palms, wrists etc) at chest level.

Objective 2 Beat your previous record.

Advice 1 Legs must be kept steady.

Advice 2 Develop confidence in the goalkeepers.

Coaching Point
Encourage the goalkeepers to count the number of touches they make with the ball.

A — BALL FAMILIARITY

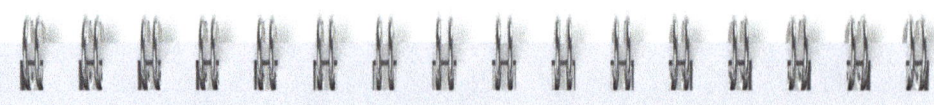

DRILL 2 — BALL IN THE AIR (OVER THE HEAD) WITH STABLE LEGS (LEVEL 1)

Objective 1 In this drill the goalkeeper must hold the ball in the air over his head. Eyes must be focused on the ball at all times.

Objective 2 The goalkeeper must use his fingers. It is very important that he keeps his fingers flexible in order to control the ball with ease.

Advice 1 Legs must be kept steady.

Advice 2 Develop confidence in the goalkeepers.

Coaching Points

1. Keep wrists stable and fingers flexible.
2. Always keep eyes focused on the ball.

DRILL 3   **VARIOUS DRILLS WITH HANDS (BALL IN THE AIR) WITH MOVEMENT (LEVEL 1)**

Objective 1 In this drill, the goalkeepers use a combination of contacts (palm, wrist, fist etc.).

Objective 2 They work at medium and high level.

Advice The goalkeeper can move freely or in specific directions.

Coaching Points

1. Encourage the goalkeepers to use various techniques.
2. Count the number of touches they make with the ball.

A   BALL FAMILIARITY

4a drill

DRILL 4A — BALL IN THE AIR WITH PUNCHES AND STEADY LEGS (LEVEL 1)

Objective 1 The goalkeepers use their fists to punch and keep the ball in the air.

Objective 2 They keep their punches steady and the ball in their visual zone.

Advice 1 Legs must be kept steady.

Advice 2 Do not use strength.

Coaching Point It is very important that the surface of the fist is level and that the fingers are not too closed or tight.

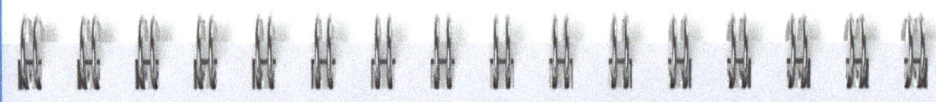

DRILL 4B — BALL IN THE AIR WITH PUNCHES AND MOVEMENT (LEVEL 2)

Once the goalkeepers have become familiar with the Drill 4a, then we move onto advanced variations.

Coaching Point The goalkeepers use their punches to keep the ball in the air while at the same time they kneel, lie down and return to a standing position while controlling the ball.

Coaching Point It is very important that the surface of the fist is flat and the fingers are not too closed or tight.

BALL FAMILIARITY

DRILL 5 — ROTATING THE BALL (LEVEL 1)

Objective 1 Rotate the ball around the upper body in both directions.

Objective 2 Pass the ball through the legs in the air and on the ground (figure of eight).

Objective 3 Rotate the ball around the upper body and the legs in a combination of movements. This will develop the goalkeeper's confidence and his familiarity with the ball.

DRILL 6A   QUICK HAND WORK - A (LEVEL 2)

Description Place one hand in front of the legs and one behind, holding the ball. Quickly change the position of the hands, while simultaneously gripping the ball without dropping it.

Advice Legs should be slightly bent.

A BALL FAMILIARITY

DRILL 6B   **QUICK HAND WORK - B (LEVEL 2)**

Description Place hands in front of legs while holding the ball (image 1). Quickly change the position of the hands while simultaneously transferring the ball (through the legs) from the front to behind the legs.

Advice Legs should be slightly bent.

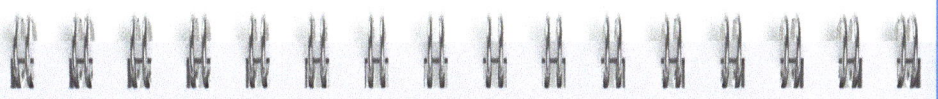

DRILL 7   DYNAMIC STRETCHING WITH THE BALL (LEVEL 1)

Description The goalkeeper holds the ball with his left hand and completes a sideways stretch of the upper body, while transferring the ball with as much distance as possible from his body. He then does the same with his right hand and repeats.

Advice 1 Smooth and rhythmic transfers from one hand to the other.

Advice 2 Repeat this action in all directions and from varied heights.

A BALL FAMILIARITY

DRILL 8 — DYNAMIC STRETCHING WITH THE BALL (LEVEL 1)

Description The goalkeeper keeps his legs steady. He holds the ball in front of him at a low level. He lifts the ball with his left hand over his body and his head. He then repeats the same with the other hand.

Advice 1 Smooth and rhythmic transfers from one hand to the other.

Advice 2 Arms should be stretched and straight.

DRILL 9A COLLECTING THE BALL WITH SINGLE HAND AND STEADY LEGS (LEVEL 1)

Description The goalkeeper holds the ball with his left hand on the right side of his body. He then places it on the ground and immediately collects it with the right hand as soon as it touches the ground. He then repeats the same exercise, starting with the right hand and collecting with the left hand.

Advice 1 Steady legs in a stretching position.

Advice 2 Arms should be stretched and straight.

Advice 3 Dynamic motion.

A BALL FAMILIARITY

DRILL 9B — CATCHING THE BALL SINGLE-HANDED WHILE MOVING (LEVEL 1)

Description The goalkeeper is holding the ball with his left hand at the right part of his body. He then drops the ball, only to catch it with his right hand as soon as it touches the ground. Afterwards, he does the same with the opposite hands.

Advice 1 The goalkeeper moves left or right in parallel.

Advice 2 His hands must be fully extended during the drill.

Advice 3 Explosive movement.

DRILL 10A CATCHING THE BALL SINGLE-HANDED WITH FIXED LEGS (LEVEL 1)

Description The goalkeeper holds the ball with his left hand on the left part of his body. He then lets the ball drop, only to catch the ball with the same hand as soon as it touches the ground. Afterwards, he does the same with the opposite hands and repeats.

Advice 1 Fixed legs in stretching position.

Advice 2 His hands must be fully extended during the drill.

Advice 3 Explosive movement.

A BALL FAMILIARITY

DRILL 10B — COLLECTING THE BALL WITH SINGLE HAND AND MOVEMENT (LEVEL 1)

Description 1 The goalkeeper holds the ball with his left hand on the left side of his body (image 1). He drops the ball and immediately collects it with the same hand as soon as it touches the ground (image 2). In contrast to previous page, the goalkeeper can now move and does not have to stay static. Afterwards, he does the same with the opposite hands and repeats.

Description 2 The goalkeeper moves (runs) towards different directions.

Advice 1 Transfer center of gravity towards the direction of movement

Advice 2 Rhythm.

Advice 3 Dynamic motion.

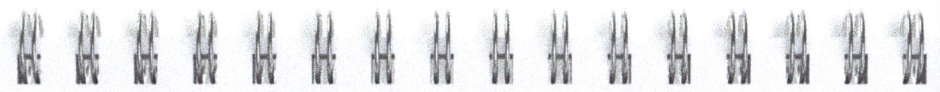

DRILL 11   SINGLE HAND CATCHES ABOVE THE WAIST (LEVEL 1)

Description The goalkeeper throws the ball with his right hand above his head (images 1-2). At the same time, the goalkeeper moves slightly backwards and catches the ball with the other hand (image 3). Repeat with opposite hands.

Advice 1 Legs move sideways.

Advice 2 Change the position of the upper body while moving (without taking steps backwards).

A   BALL FAMILIARITY

DRILL 12 — THROWING AND CATCHING WITH MOVEMENT (LEVEL 1)

Description The goalkeeper runs in specified space. He holds the ball with his hands and throws it on the ground (image 1-2) and then catches it with a grip (image 3-4)

Advice Correct positioning of hands on ball.

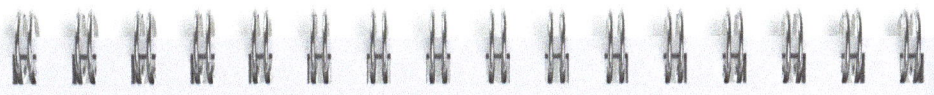

DRILL 13   THROWING AND CATCHING WITH JUMP (LEVEL 1)

Description The goalkeeper runs into a specified space. He holds the ball with his hands and throws it in the air and then catches it with a grip and small jump.

Advice 1 The ball is thrown at medium height.

Advice 2 Monitor the correct positioning of the hands on the ball.

A BALL FAMILIARITY

DRILL 14 — TRANSFERING AND COLLECTING THE BALL (LEVEL 1)

Description The goalkeeper runs into a specified space. He holds the ball with his hands and rolls it on the ground (image 1) with one hand at a time. He then runs to catch it (image 2-3).

Advice 1 Correct foot positioning. The back foot should be on the side of the ball and not behind it.

Advice 2 Good flow of movement.

Advice 3 Collect the ball with your forward force.

DRILL 15 ROLL WITH THE BALL (LEVEL 1)

Description The goalkeeper rolls with the ball ('forward roll) in his hands and returns to a standing position without losing his grip of the ball.

Advice Balance and flexibility.

BALL FAMILIARITY

DRILL 16 — THROWING AND CATCHING WITH FALL (LEVEL 1)

Description The goalkeeper throws the ball in the air (images 1-2) and catches it with a fall as it lands on the ground (images 3-5).

Advice 1-2 Correct foot positioning to get hands to ball. Good flow of movement.

Advice 3 Move your leg in the same direction of the fall for support & boost.

Goalkeeper Training Methodology

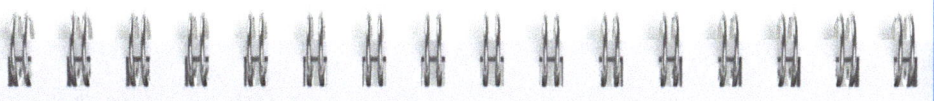

DRILL 17 FOOTWORK WITH THE BALL (LEVEL 1)

Description The goalkeeper performs continuous touches with the ball between his feet by using the insides of his feet (side-to-side).

Advice 1 Maintain good rhythm.

Advice 2 Maintain good body posture.

Coaching Point Repeat while steady and in motion.

A BALL FAMILIARITY

DRILL 18 FOOTWORK WITH THE BALL - SAMBA (LEVEL 1)

Description This is a variation of the previous page, as the goalkeeper performs the side-to-side touches as though he is dancing Samba.

Advice 1 Maintain good rhythm.

Advice 2 Maintain good body posture.

Advice 3 The supporting leg makes a double bounce to provide the rhythm.

DRILL 19   **FOOTWORK WITH THE BALL – STEPS (LEVEL 1)**

Description The goalkeeper performs continuous touches with the ball using the tips of his toes on the top of the ball.

Advice 1 Correct body posture and hand motion.

Advice 2 Repeat while steady and while moving back to front.

Advice 3 Maintain good rhythm.

A   BALL FAMILIARITY

drill 20a

DRILL 20A   **FOOTWORK WITH THE BALL – INSIDE OF FOOT (LEVEL 1)**

Description   The goalkeeper throws the ball in the air with his hands (images 1-2). As soon as the ball hits the ground, he controls it using the inside of his foot (images 3-4). Make sure to alternate, using both feet.

While maintaining control of the ball, he will move left or right with the ball, depending on which foot he controls the ball with.

Advice 1   Be ready before the ball is thrown into the air.

Advice 2   Place center of gravity towards the direction of motion.

Advice 3   The ball is dropped from a low height.

Advice 4   Keep your eyes on the ball.

Goalkeeper Training Methodology

DRILL 20B FOOTWORK WITH THE BALL – OUTSIDE OF FOOT (LEVEL 1)

Description The goalkeeper throws the ball in the air with his hands (images 1-2). As soon as the ball hits the ground, he controls it by using the outside of his foot (image 3). Make sure to alternate, using both feet.

While maintaining control of the ball, he will move left or right with the ball, depending on which foot he controls the ball with.

Advice 1 Be ready before the ball is thrown into the air.

Advice 2 Place center of gravity towards the direction of motion.

Advice 3 The ball is dropped from a low height.

Advice 4 Keep your eyes on the ball.

A BALL FAMILIARITY

drill 21a

DRILL 21A TURNING WITH THE BALL – INSIDE OF FOOT (LEVEL 1)

Description The goalkeeper throws the ball in the air and backwards with his hands (images 1-2). At the same time, he turns 180 degrees (image 3) and as soon as the ball hits the ground, he controls it with the inside of his foot (images 4-5).

While maintaining control of the ball, he will return to his initial position and repeat the exercise with the opposite foot.

Advice 1 Be ready before the ball is thrown into air.

Advice 2 Place center of gravity towards the direction of motion.

Advice 3 Keep your eyes on the ball.

DRILL 21B TURNING WITH THE BALL – OUTSIDE OF FOOT (LEVEL 1)

Description The goalkeeper throws the ball in the air and backwards with his hands (images 1-2). At the same time, he turns 180 degrees (image 3) and as soon as the ball hits the ground, he controls it with the outside of his foot (image 3).

While maintaining control of the ball, he will return to his initial position and repeat the exercise with the opposite foot.

Advice 1 Center of gravity towards direction of motion.

Advice 2 Use both feet.

Advice 3 Keep your eyes on the ball.

A BALL FAMILIARITY

CHAPTER 2

LEARNING THE BASIC PRINCIPLES

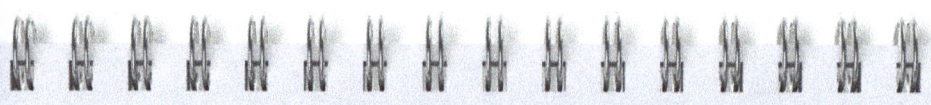

DRILL 1   **STEPS: FORWARD MOVEMENT (LEVEL 1)**

Description The goalkeeper moves forward stepping over obstacles (balls or cones).

The goalkeeper must keep his body steady and his arms should move in coordination with his legs.

Advice 1 Maintain a good rhythm.

Advice 2 The knees should be lifted in front of the body.

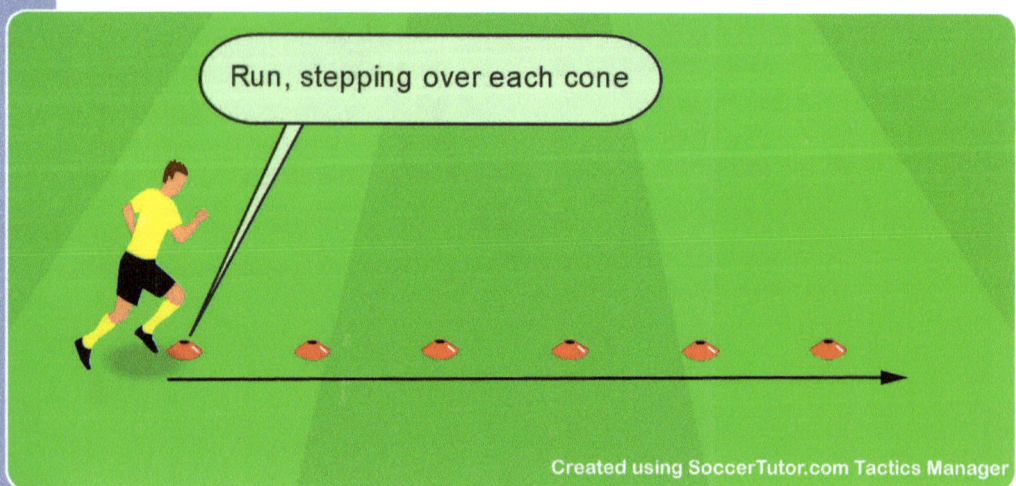

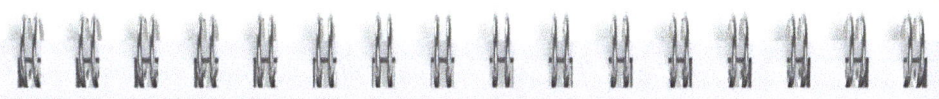

DRILL 2   STEPS: SIDEWAYS MOVEMENT (LEVEL 1)

Description The goalkeeper moves sideways between obstacles (balls or cones).

The goalkeeper must keep his body steady.

Advice 1 Maintain a good rhythm and make sure that your body weight is kept forward.

Advice 2 Take many small steps and make contact with the ground as frequently as possible.

If you pay attention to the basic steps, successful catches of the ball will naturally follow

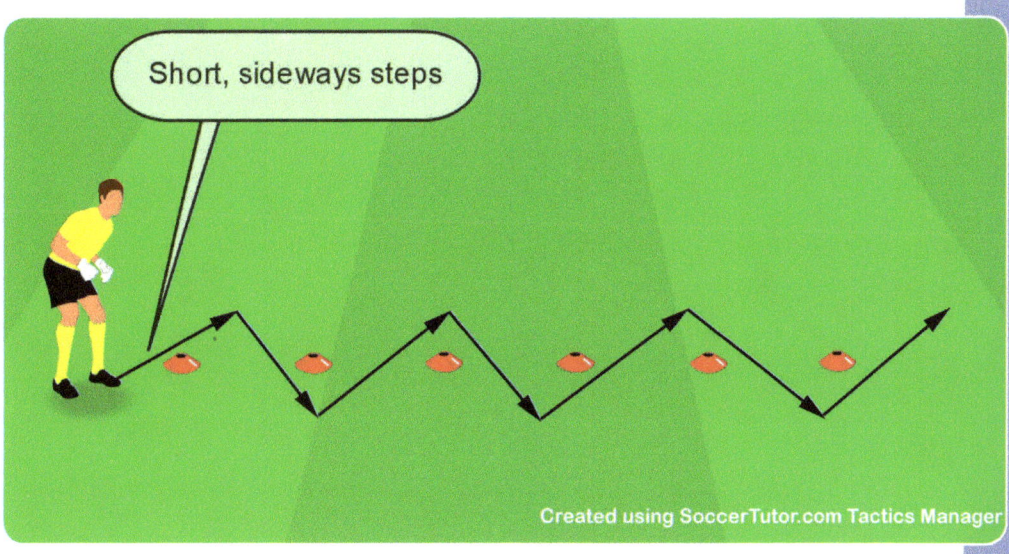

B LEARNING THE BASIC PRINCIPLES

DRILL 3 — STEPS: FORWARD AND BACKWARD MOVEMENT (LEVEL 1)

Description The goalkeeper moves forward and backwards between obstacles (balls or cones).

Advice 1 Take many small steps. The body weight should interchange back and forth based on the direction of the steps.

Advice 2 Simulate steps made in a competitive match.

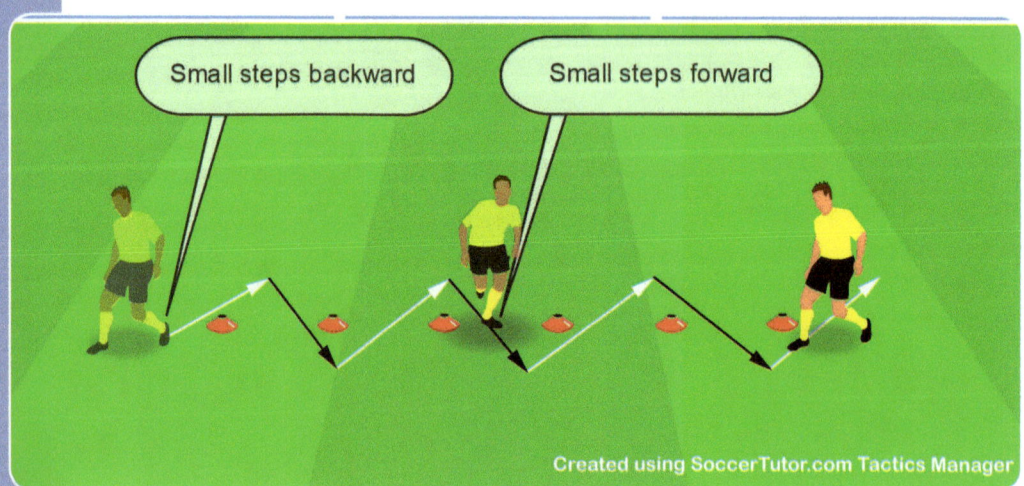

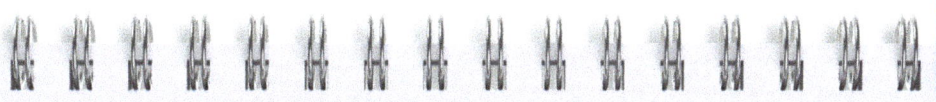

DRILL 4   **STEPS: SIDEWAYS MOVEMENT-KNEE LIFTS (LEVEL 1)**

Description The goalkeeper moves sideways over 6-8 obstacles (balls or cones).

Move naturally. The body must be kept steady and the arms should move in coordination with the legs.

Advice Take two steps between each cone.

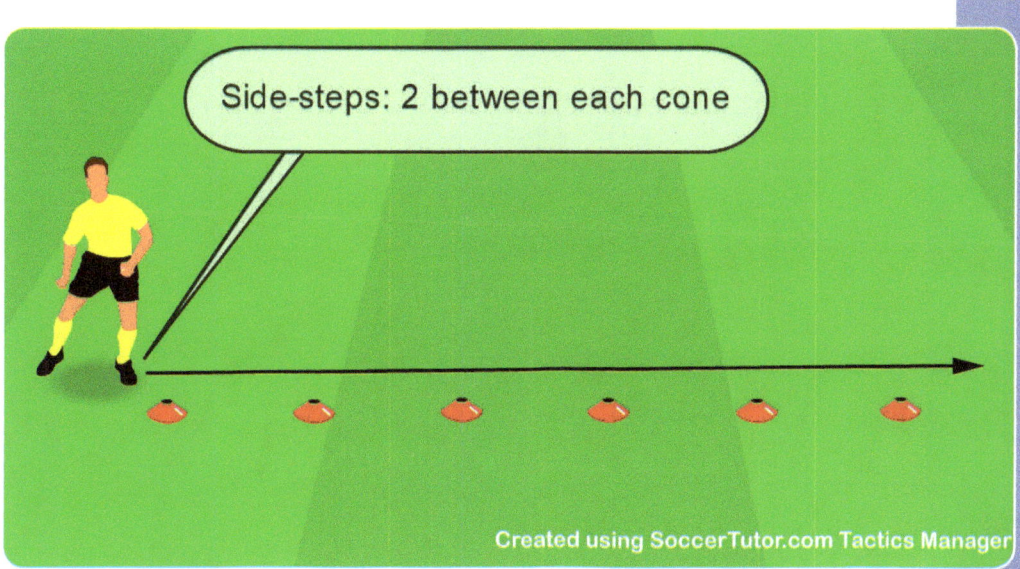

B   LEARNING THE BASIC PRINCIPLES

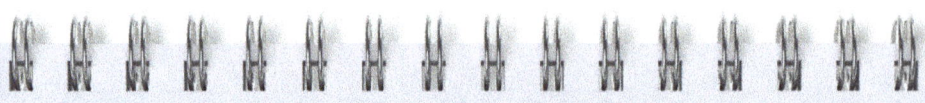

DRILL 5   JUMPS WITH TWO FEET (LEVEL 1)

Description The goalkeeper jumps over obstacles (balls or cones) with both feet.

Advice 1 Legs should be set apart at shoulder width.

Advice 2 Knees should be positioned forward during the jump.

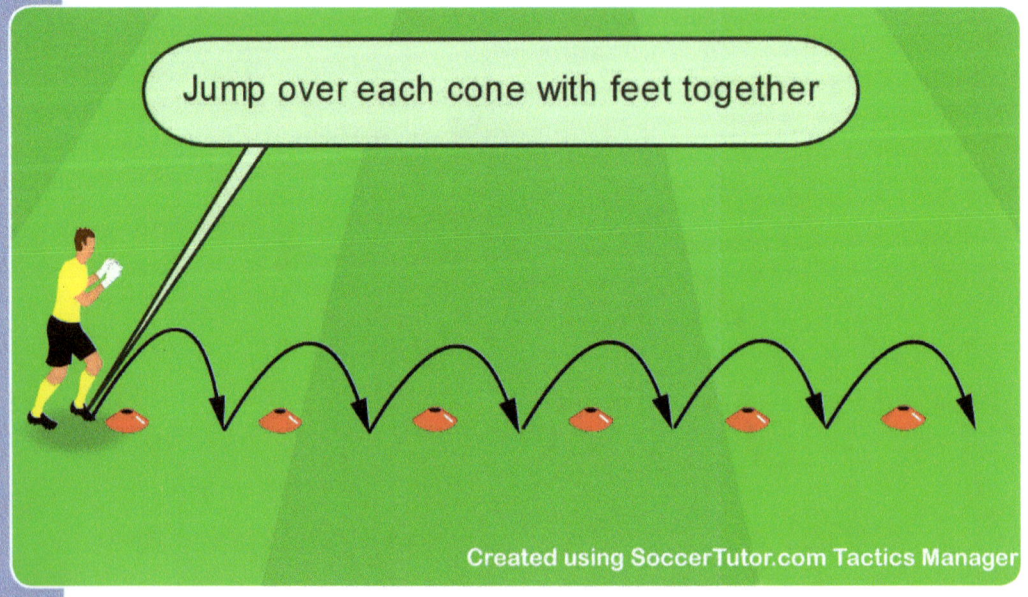

Jump over each cone with feet together

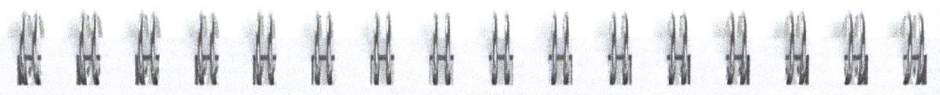

DRILL 6 — JUMPS WITH ALTERNATING SINGLE FOOT (LEVEL 1)

Description The goalkeeper jumps over obstacles (balls or cones) while alternating feet. He hops from left foot and then to right foot each time.

Advice Knees should be positioned forward during the jump.

Jump at maximum height

LEARNING THE BASIC PRINCIPLES

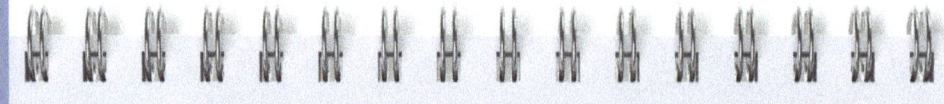

DRILL 7   JUMPS AT MAXIMUM HEIGHT WITH TWO FEET (LEVEL 1)

Description The goalkeeper jumps over obstacles (balls or cones) with both feet.

The goalkeeper must jump at the maximum possible height.

Advice 1 Legs should be set apart at shoulder width.

Advice 2 Dynamic jump.

Advice 3 Knees should be positioned forward during the jump.

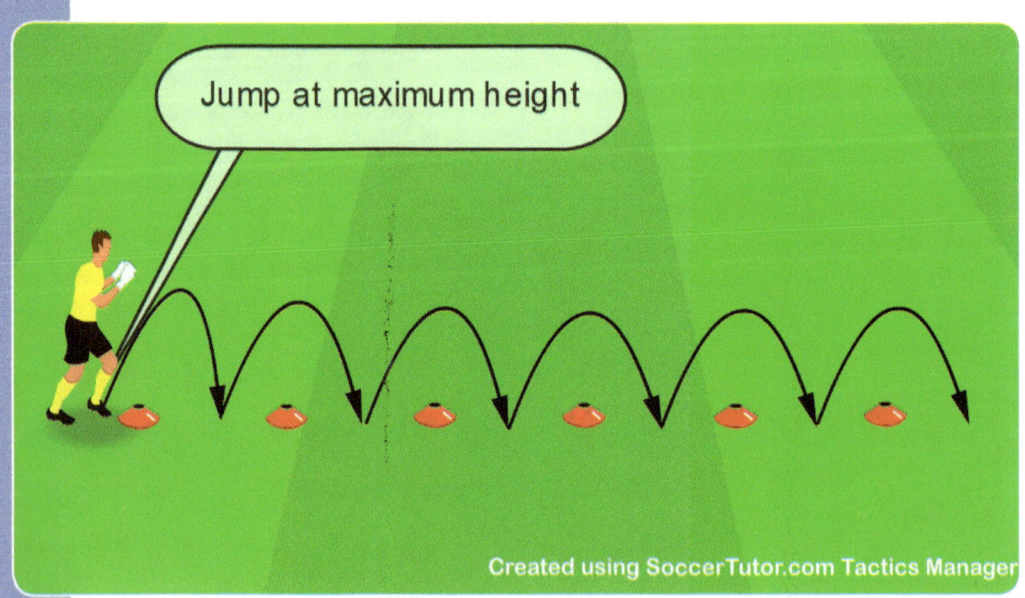

DRILL 8   STEPS WITH ROTATION (LEVEL 1)

Description The goalkeeper takes steps sideways while rotating around an obstacle (ball or cone).

Advice 1 The direction of the rotation should change every 3 seconds.

Advice 2 Take many small steps. Keep body weight forward.

Side-steps around cone changing direction every 3 seconds

LEARNING THE BASIC PRINCIPLES

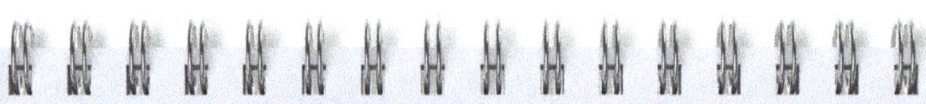

DRILL 9 — STEPS, SIDEWAYS (LEVEL 1)

Description The goalkeeper takes sideways steps around obstacles (balls or cones) positioned in a zig-zag formation as shown.

Advice 1 Take many small steps. Keep body weight forward.

Advice 2 Always be prepared to react (defend). The head must be held high and hands steady in a state of readiness.

Advice 3 Maintain good balance.

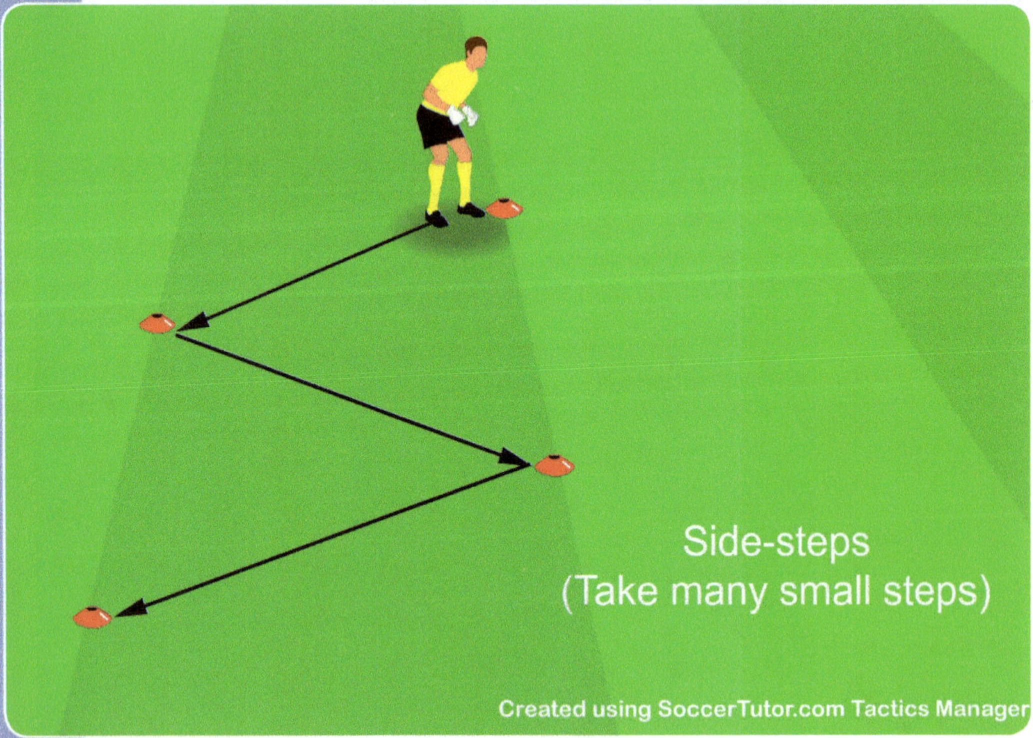

Side-steps
(Take many small steps)

DRILL 10A — HAND & FOOT COMBINATION - ONE HANDED CATCH (LEVEL 1)

Description The assistant stands 2 m. away from the goalkeeper and alternates throwing the ball to his right and left side at a medium height (abdomen height). The goalkeeper takes sideways steps and catches the ball with one hand and then returns to perform the drill on the other side.

The speed in which the drill is executed adjusts to the rhythm with which the ball is thrown.

Advice 1 Take correct sideways steps.

Advice 2 It is important that the body is placed in a forward position and that the knees are bent.

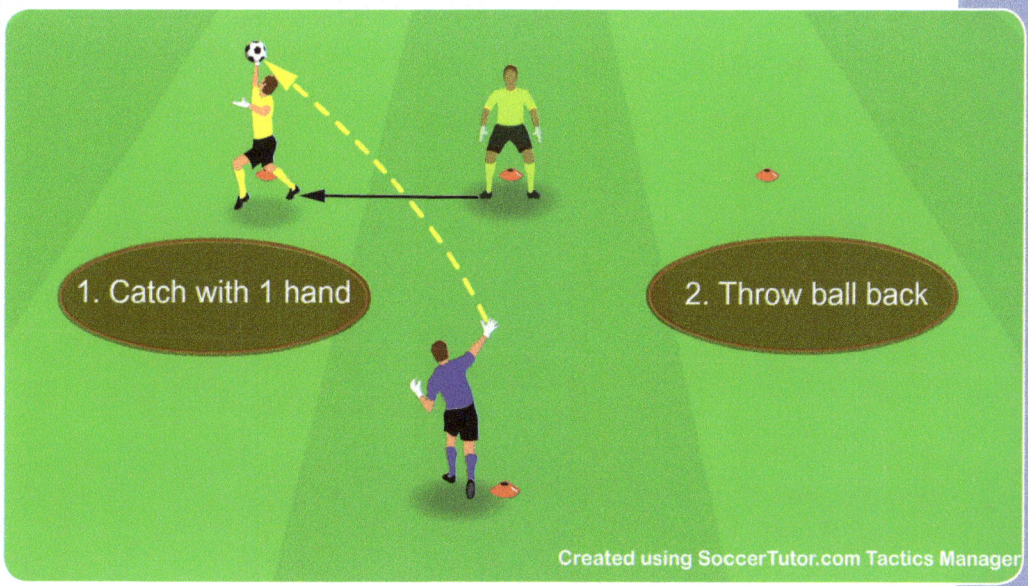

1. Catch with 1 hand
2. Throw ball back

B LEARNING THE BASIC PRINCIPLES

DRILL 10B — HAND & FOOT COMBINATION- ONE HANDED CATCH (LEVEL 2)

Description In order to intensify the level of the drill, the assistant uses two balls. He stands 2 m. away from the goalkeeper and alternates between throwing one ball to his right and then one ball to his left at a medium height (abdomen height). The goalkeeper takes sideways steps and catches each ball with the appropriate hand.

Variation Switch the order of the direction in which the balls are thrown e.g. 2-3 throws in the same direction.

Advice 1 The speed in which the drill is executed adjusts to the rhythm with which the ball is thrown.

Advice 2 Take correct sideways steps. It is important that the body is placed in a forward position and that the knees are bent.

Coaching Points
1. Move along an imaginary line. Legs should be set apart at shoulder width.
2. Movements should be fast.

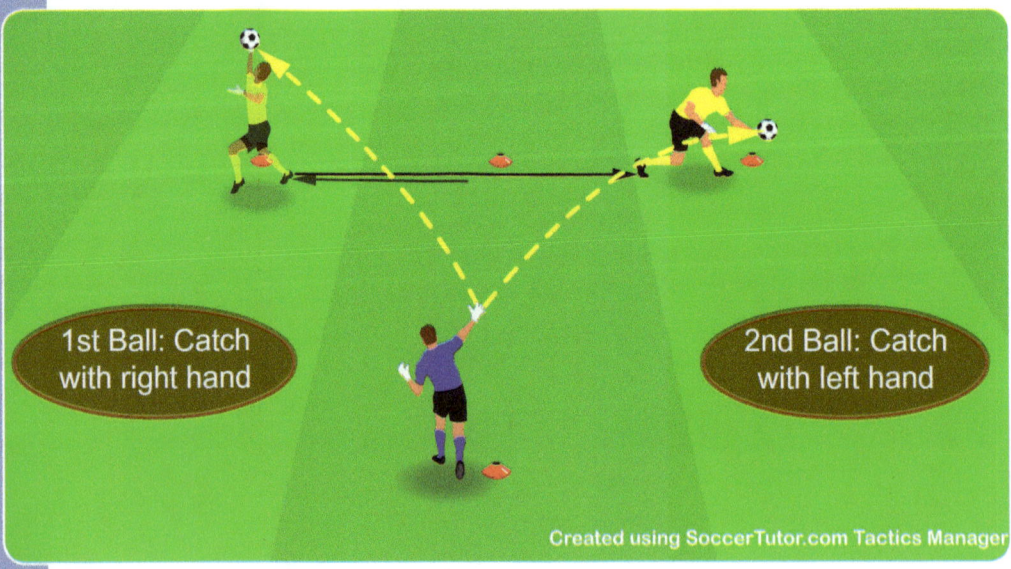

1st Ball: Catch with right hand

2nd Ball: Catch with left hand

DRILL 10C HAND & FOOT COMBINATION (LEVEL 2)

Description The assistant and the goalkeeper each hold one ball in their hands and are at a close distance to each other.

They exchange fast throws while the goalkeeper takes single sideways steps. He catches the ball and throws it back with both hands.

Advice 1 Take correct sideways steps. It is important that the body is placed in a forward position and that the knees are bent.

Advice 2 Move along an imaginary line. Legs should be set apart at shoulder width. Hand movements should be fast.

Advice 3 Fast leg movements are needed.

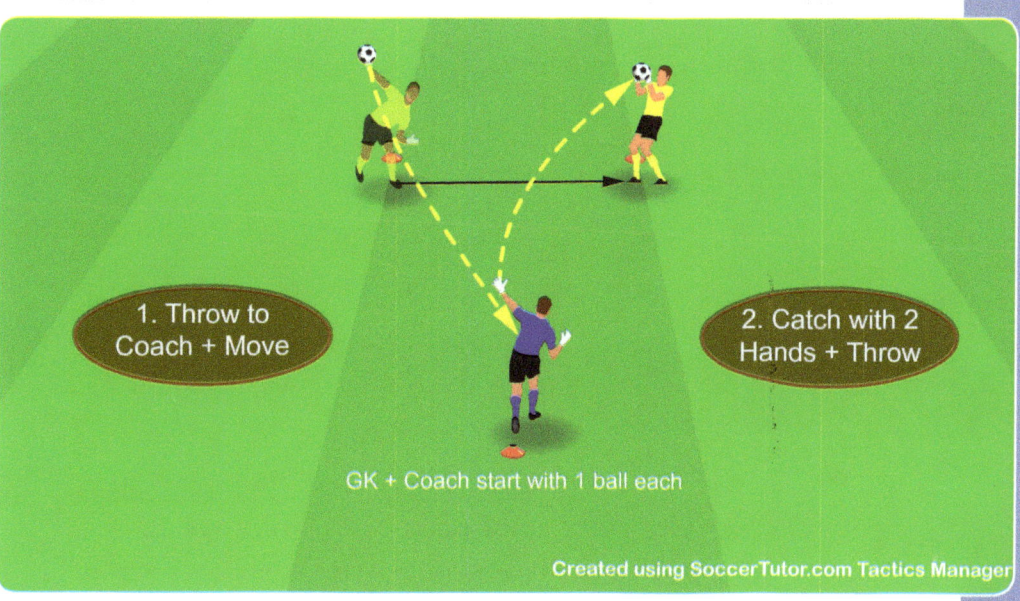

LEARNING THE BASIC PRINCIPLES

DRILL 11 — HAND & FOOT COMBINATION - SQUARE (LEVEL 2)

Description The goalkeeper stands in a square space (2 m. x 2 m.). The assistant stands at a 2 m. distance with a ball in his hands.

The assistant serves the ball to the goalkeeper towards various points within the square. He serves the ball low and high.

The goalkeeper must use the right steps in order to move back and forth and catch the ball. Repeat 8-10 times.

Advice 1 The ball must not touch the ground.

Advice 2 The goalkeeper must not move outside the designated square space (2 m. x 2 m.).

Coaching Points

1. Legs must move fast and the head must be steady.
2. Use the correct grip in order to catch the ball.

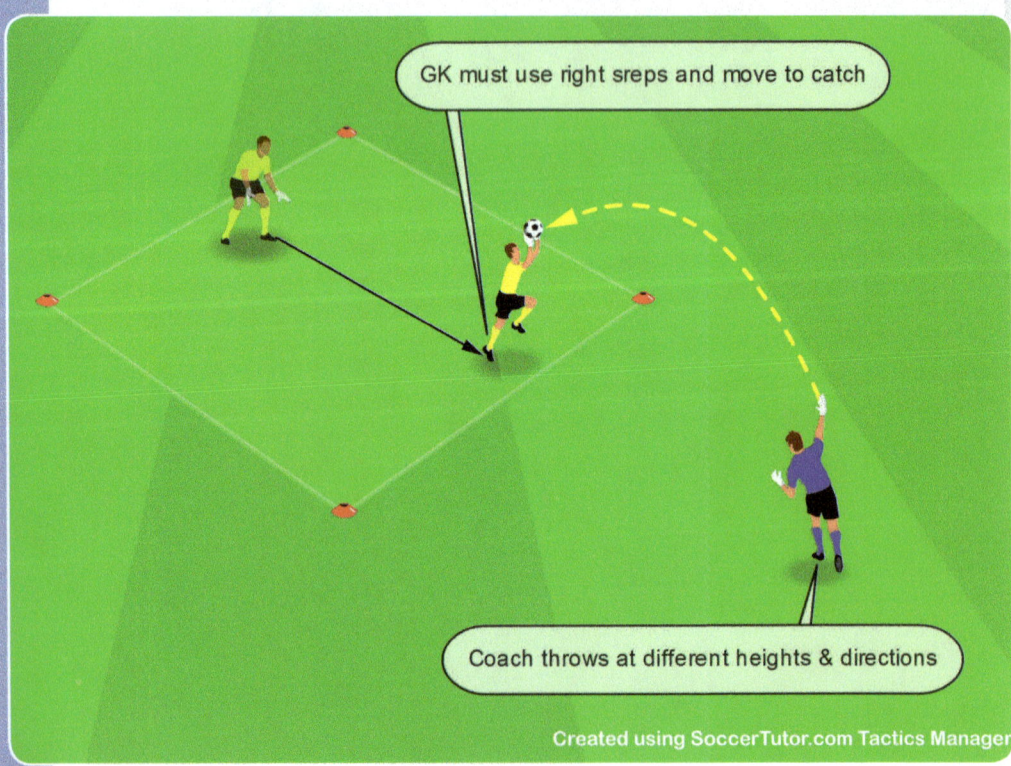

GK must use right sreps and move to catch

Coach throws at different heights & directions

CHAPTER 3

INTRODUCTION TO HANDLING TECHNIQUES

The common catch for the goalkeeper is what receiving is to the outfield player. That is why the goalkeeper must always improve this very important skill.

There are three types of catches: The low grip "K", the grip in the abdominal area "C" and the grip at the height of the chest and above called "W". In this chapter the drills will cover all three types of catches.

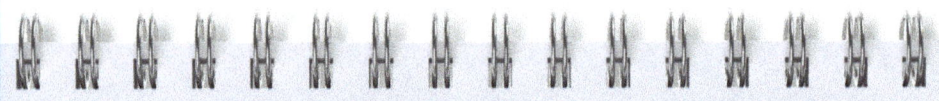

DRILL 1   CATCH "K" ON KNEES (LEVEL 1)

The low catch "K" is suggested for close low passes that are directed towards the goalkeeper.

Description The goalkeeper is on his knees. The assistant is approximately 2 m. away and passes straight low balls directed towards him.

Advice 1 He collects the ball with both hands

Advice 2 Hands are properly placed on the ball and then secured into the body.

Advice 3 He returns the ball with both hands by rolling it on the ground.

Coaching Points 1. Hands are positioned behind the ball.
2. The ball rolls into the hands, and is then secured into the body.

Goalkeeper Training Methodology

DRILL 2   **CATCH "C" ON KNEES (LEVEL 1)**

The medium catch "C" is suggested for close balls that are directed towards the abdominal area of the goalkeeper.

Description The goalkeeper is on his knees (image 1). The assistant is approximately 2 m. away and passes straight balls directed towards the abdominal area.

Advice 1 He collects the ball in the abdominal area with both hands (image 2).

Advice 2 Hands are properly placed behind the ball and then secured on the body (image 3).

Advice 3 He returns the ball with both hands by rolling it on the ground.

INTRODUCTION TO HANDLING TECHNIQUES

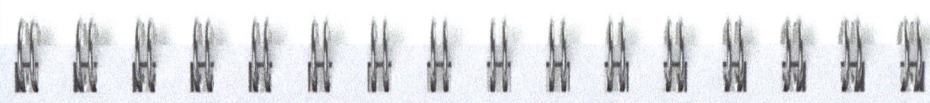

DRILL 3   CATCH "W" SITTING POSITION (LEVEL 1)

The "W" catch is suggested when the balls are passed at the height of the chest and above. The goalkeeper uses this grip to catch the ball and then to secure it to his body (stability-security).

Description The goalkeeper is in a sitting position (image 1) and receives the ball from the assistant at the height of his chest and at various points around his body (images 2-3).

Advice The goalkeeper catches the ball with the use of his palm and fingers.

Coaching Points 1. Hands must be steady and eyes fixed on the ball. 2. Use forearms to absorb the force of ball. 3. Collect and bring the ball to the chest.

DRILL 4 — CATCH "W" ON KNEES (LEVEL 1)

Description The goalkeeper is on his knees and receives the ball from the assistant at various points around his body (images 2-3).

Advice 1 The goalkeeper catches the ball with the use of his palm and fingers.

Advice 2 He returns the ball by throwing it with one hand (pass). Alternate using the left and right hand (one at a time).

Coaching Points The same as the previous drill (drill 3).

INTRODUCTION TO HANDLING TECHNIQUES

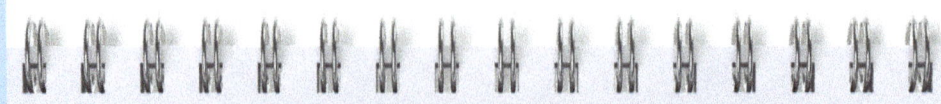

DRILL 5   **CATCH DECISION MAKING ON KNESS (LEVEL 1)**

Description The goalkeeper is on his knees and receives the ball from the assistant at various points around his body.

The assistant throws the ball in various places in order to force the goalkeeper to make the right decision as to which grip technique to use in order to catch the ball.

Advice 1 Eyes must be fixed on the ball at all times.

Advice 2 Use the correct grip for each different serve by choosing between catches "K", "C" or "W" (explained on previous pages).

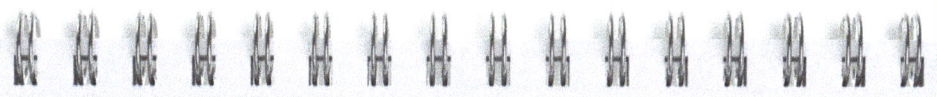

DRILL 6   **DECISION MAKING FROM STANDING POSITION (LEVEL 1)**

Description The goalkeeper is in a standing position (image 1) and is served balls from the assistant at various points around or at his body from a 5 m. distance. The goalkeeper must decide which grip technique he must use in order to catch each ball (images 2-4 on next page).

Advice 1 Use catches "K" or "C" for passes at chest level and below. Use grip "W" for passes above the chest.

Advice 2 Always take steps forward and NEVER backwards.

Advice 3 Always wait for the ball to leave the assistant's feet before you react.

Coaching Points

1. Legs are set apart at shoulder width and knees are bent.
2. Body weight is placed forward and the eyes are fixed on the ball at all times.
3. Hands are in a state of readiness and always stand on the tips of the toes.

INTRODUCTION TO HANDLING TECHNIQUES

drill 6

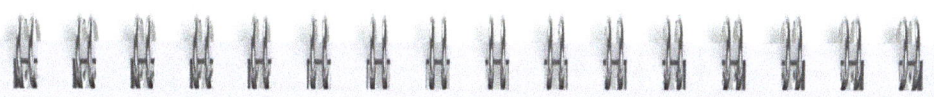

DRILL 7   CATCH AWAY FROM THE BODY (LEVEL 1)

Description Two goalkeepers stand 8 m. apart and pass the ball to one another at various points around them.

The objective is for the goalkeepers use their feet and body correctly, before making the right choice of catch for each throw.

Advice 1 Be in a state of readiness before the catch.

Advice 2 It is important that the feet move correctly so that the goalkeeper's body is in the right position at the right moment, in order to successfully catch the ball.

Advice 3 This drill helps develop the goalkeeper's catching ability and increases his self-confidence.

Coaching Points The same as the previous drill.

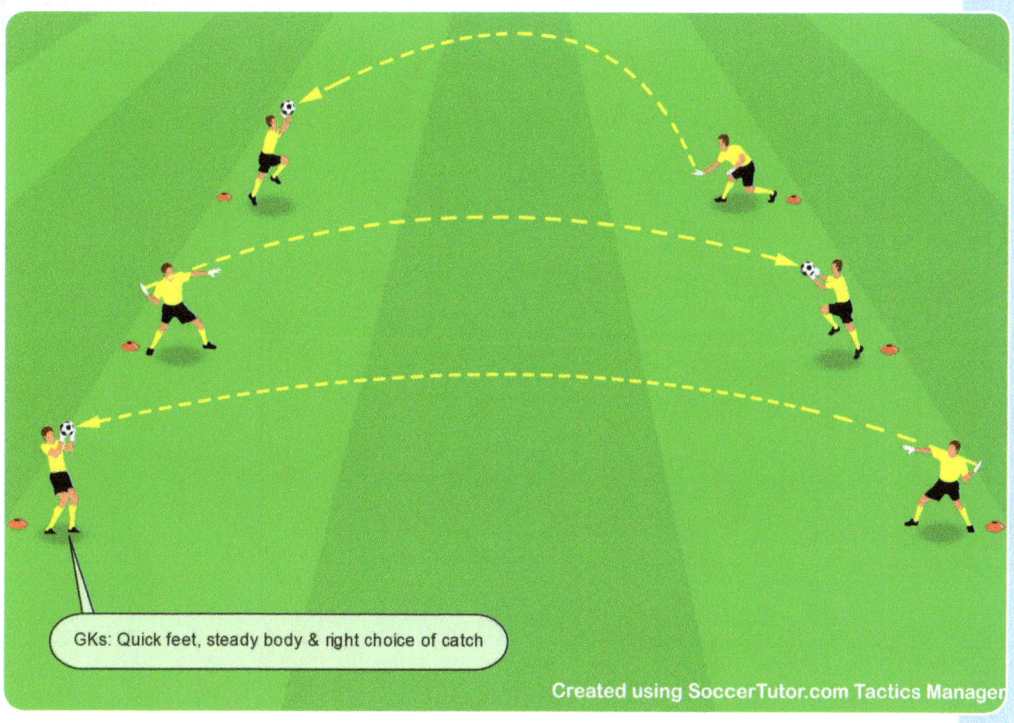

GKs: Quick feet, steady body & right choice of catch

INTRODUCTION TO HANDLING TECHNIQUES

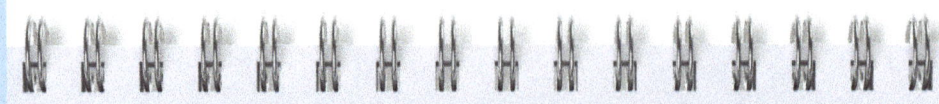

DRILL 8   CATCHES WITH EXTENDED ARM (LEVEL 1)

Description The goalkeeper in a sitting position and the assistant passes balls to his right and to his left, with the aim to catch with an extended arm. The goalkeeper must grip with his right hand as he falls left, and with his left hand as he halls to the right.

Advice 1 Always wait for the ball to leave the assistant before you react.

Advice 2 Eyes must be fixed on the ball at all times.

DRILL 9 — SINGLE HAND CATCH - SITTING POSITION (LEVEL 2)

Description The goalkeeper in a sitting position and the assistant passes balls close to his body with force. The goalkeeper must try to read the flight of the ball, adjust and control the balls with single hand catches.

Advice 1 This drill develops the goalkeeper self-confidence in his handling technique.

Advice 2 Eyes must be fixed on the ball at all times.

INTRODUCTION TO HANDLING TECHNIQUES

DRILL 10A SINGLE HAND CATCH - STANDING POSITION (LEVEL 1)

Description Two goalkeepers stand 5 m. apart and throw the ball to one another with their hands high and with force.

The goalkeepers must try to catch the balls with a single hand.

Advice 1 Be in a state of readiness before the catch.

Advice 2 It is important that the feet move correctly so that the goalkeeper's body is in the right position at the right moment, in order to successfully catch the ball.

Coaching Points

1. The position of the body must quickly align with the direction of the ball.

2. The head must be held steady and the force of the ball should be absorbed.

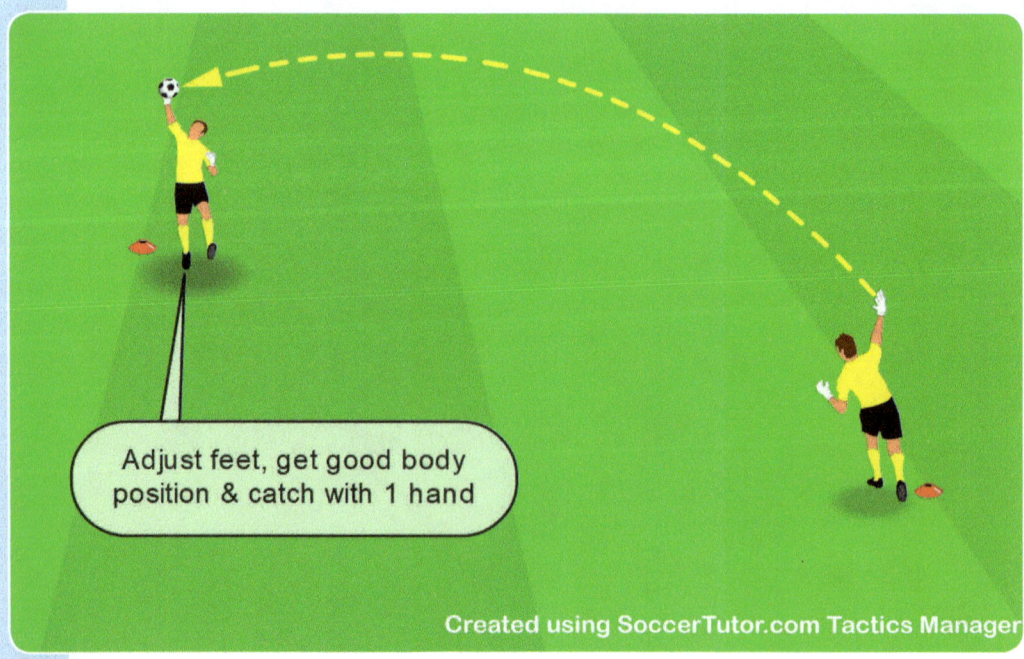

Adjust feet, get good body position & catch with 1 hand

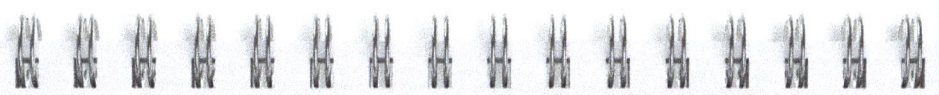

DRILL 10B SINGLE HAND CATCH - TWO BALLS (LEVEL 2)

Description Two goalkeepers stand 3 m. apart and each of them hold one ball in opposite hands.

They simultaneously throw the balls to each other and catch them with the opposite hand they were thrown with.

Advice 1 Maintain good rhythm.

Advice 2 Feet must work fast.

Advice 3 It is important that the feet move correctly so that the goalkeeper's body is in the right position at the right moment, in order to successfully catch the ball.

Simultaneous with 2 balls:
Throw with 1 hand, catch with other

INTRODUCTION TO HANDLING TECHNIQUES

DRILL 10C SINGLE HAND CATCH - HIGH SPEED (LEVEL 3)

Description Two goalkeepers stand 7 m. apart and throw a ball to each other with force.

The goalkeepers must try to catch the ball with a single hand.

Advice 1 Be in a state of readiness before the catch.

Advice 2 It is important that the feet move correctly so that the goalkeeper's body is in the right position at the right moment, in order to successfully catch the ball.

Coaching Points

1. The position of the body must quickly align with the direction of the ball.
2. The head must be held steady and the force of the ball should be absorbed (soft hands).

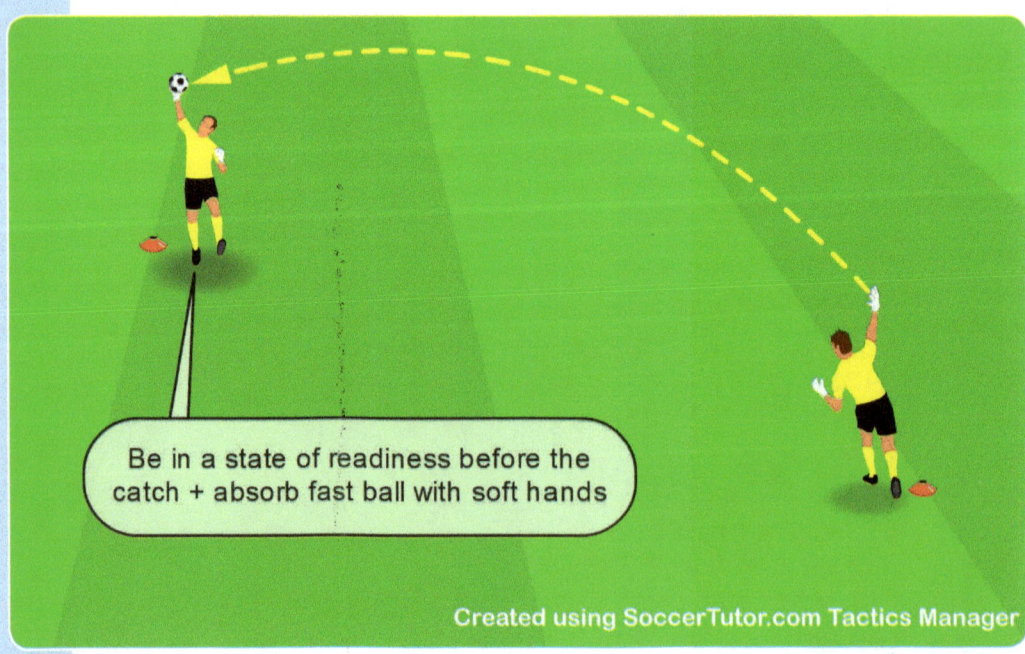

Be in a state of readiness before the catch + absorb fast ball with soft hands

CHAPTER 4

SHOT STOPPING

In order for the goalkeeper to react to shots, he must be in the right position at the right moment. He needs to be fast on his feet and use the correct grip technique. In the following drills we will be faced with a variety of circumstances in which excellent technique must be combined with the correct decision making - the appropriate technique must be used for each different situation.

DRILL 1A **THE "W" CATCH (LEVEL 1)**

Description The goalkeeper is in a standing position between two cones (2 m. goal). The assistant is at a 5 m. distance. The assistant passes high balls towards the 'goal' with controlled speed. The goalkeeper must try to catch the ball with a combination of correct steps and correct use of the "W" handling technique (image 2 - described earlier in book).

Advice 1 Be in a state of readiness before the catch.

Advice 2 Move towards the ball.

Advice 3 Always position the body between the ball and the 'goal'.

Goalkeeper Training Methodology

DRILL 1B   THE "C" CATCH (LEVEL 1)

Description The goalkeeper is in a standing position between two cones (2 m. goal). The assistant is at a 5 m. distance. The assistant passes medium height balls towards the 'goal' with controlled speed. The goalkeeper must try to catch the ball with a combination of correct steps and the correct use of the "C" handling technique.

Advice The same as the previous drill.

D   SHOT STOPPING

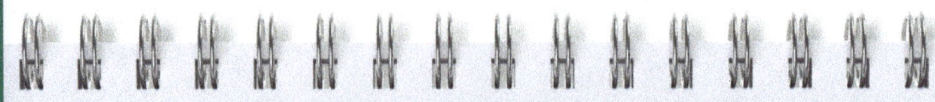

DRILL 1C   THE "K" CATCH METHOD (LEVEL 1)

This drill is the same as the previous two with the only difference being that it is combined with a footwork technique called "K" which means that one leg bends slightly.

Description The goalkeeper is in a standing position between two cones (2 m. goal). The assistant is at a 5 m. distance. The assistant passes medium height balls towards the 'goal' with controlled speed.

The goalkeeper must try to catch the ball with a combination of correct steps and correct use of the "K" handling technique.

Advice The same as the previous two drills.

Coaching Points

1. Position your legs so that the ball cannot fit between them.
2. Place your hands behind the ball. Secure the ball to your chest (security).

D SHOT STOPPING

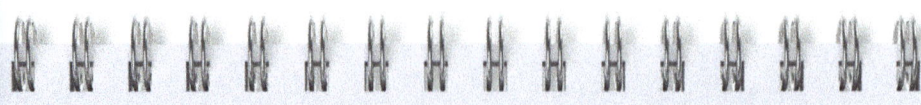

2a drill

DRILL 2A   THE WALL (LEVEL 1)

Description The goalkeeper is in a standing position between two cones (2 m. goal). The assistant is at a 5 m. distance.

The goalkeeper places his hands behind his back (image 2, inactive). The assistant passes low balls towards the 'goal' with controlled speed.

The goalkeeper must try to block the ball with the correct steps, while bending the knee onto the ground (images 3-4).

Advice 1 Be in a state of readiness.

Advice 2 Create a wall between the ball and the 'goal'.

Coaching Points

1. Bend your knee inwards.
2. Turn the other leg outwards to form an unbreakable wall.

1

Goalkeeper Training Methodology

drill 2a

SHOT STOPPING

DRILL 2B LEG WALL (LEVEL 1)

Description The goalkeeper is in a standing position between two cones (2 m. goal). The assistant is at a 5 m. distance. The goalkeeper places his hands behind his back (image 2, inactive). The assistant passes low balls towards the 'goal' with controlled speed. The goalkeeper must try to catch the ball with correct steps and by cutting off the path of the ball towards the 'goal' with his legs straight.

Advice 1 Be in a state of readiness.

Advice 2 Create a wall between the ball and the 'goal' with your legs.

Coaching Points 1. Be in a state of readiness.
2. Position your legs (close together) so that the ball does not fit between them.

Goalkeeper Training Methodology

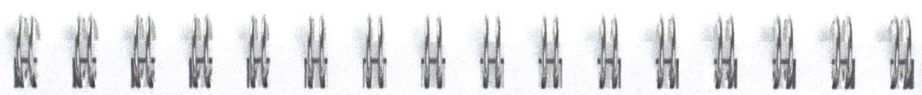

DRILL 3   **STRAIGHT LEGS AND "C" CATCH (LEVEL 1)**

Description The goalkeeper is in a standing position between two plates (2m. goal). The assistant is at a 5 m. distance. The goalkeeper places his hands behind his back. The assistant passes low balls towards the 'goal' with controlled speed. The goalkeeper must try to catch the ball with correct steps and with the correct "C" handling technique while both his legs are straight.

Advice (1) Be in a state of readiness. - (2) Move towards the ball. - (3) Always position your body between the ball and the 'goal'.

Coaching Points Position your legs so that the ball does not fit between them. Place your hands behind the ball. Secure the ball to your chest (security).

SHOT STOPPING

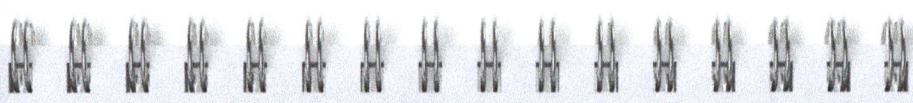

DRILL 4 — DECISION MAKING (LEVEL 1)

This drill gives the goalkeeper the opportunity to choose which of the previous techniques he will use for various passes from the assistant.

Description The goalkeeper is in a standing position between two cones (2 m. goal). The assistant is at a 5 m. distance. The assistant makes various passes towards the 'goal' with controlled speed.

The goalkeeper must decide which steps and which handling technique he will use to secure the best result (see previous pages for description of different options).

Advice 1 Be in a state of readiness.

Advice 2 Body weight must be placed forward.

Advice 3 Always wait for the ball to leave the foot or hand of the assistant before taking action.

Advice 4 Always move towards the ball.

Advice 5 Always position your body between the ball and the 'goal'.

Advice 6 Place your hands behind the ball. Secure the ball to your chest (security).

drill 4

SHOT STOPPING

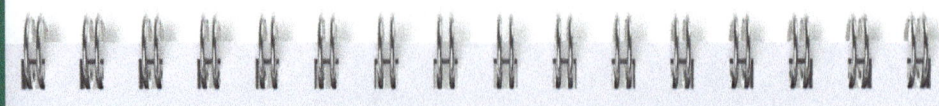

DRILL 5 — "PROTECTING THE GOAL" LOW BALLS (LEVEL 2)

The goalkeeper must predict the path of the ball in order to decide which technique is most effective to block/catch the ball.

Description The goalkeeper stands in front of a small goal. The assistant is at a 5 m. distance.

The assistant kicks low balls with controlled speed towards the goalkeeper in order to score.

Advice 1 Be in a state of readiness.

Advice 2 Body weight must be placed forward.

Advice 3 Always wait for the ball to leave the foot or hand of the assistant before taking action.

Advice 4 Always move towards the ball.

Advice 5 Always position your body between the ball and the goal.

Low shots: GK must decide what technique is best to block the ball

DRILL 6A   "PROTECTING THE GOAL" LOW GAME (LEVEL 2)

The previous drill can develop into a game of one goalkeeper against another.

Each goalkeeper must pass the ball with high force in order for the other goalkeeper to use the appropriate technique.

Description The goalkeepers stand in front of small goals (2 m. x 0.5 m.) that are positioned 10 m. apart.

The goalkeepers shoot the ball at each other with strength and speed.

The objective of this game is to score. No falls are allowed.

Advice The same as the previous drill.

Game: GKs try to score with low shots

SHOT STOPPING

DRILL 6B   PLAY "PROTECTING THE GOAL" LOW AND MEDIUM HEIGHT BALLS (LEVEL 2)

The difference from the previous drill is that the goals are now higher and the goalkeepers may also use the "C" handling technique.

Description The goalkeepers stand in front of small goals (2 m. x 1 m.) that are positioned 10 m. apart.

The goalkeepers throw or shoot the ball at each other with strength and speed. They can bounce the ball, as shown in the diagram.

The objective of this game is to use the appropriate handling technique ("C" or "K") while the opponent is trying to score. No falls are allowed.

Advice The same as the previous two drills.

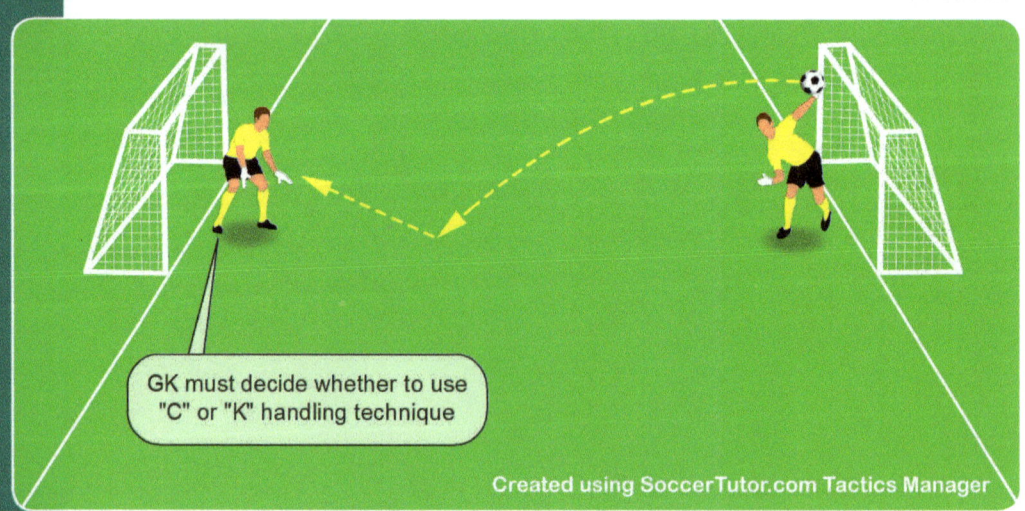

GK must decide whether to use "C" or "K" handling technique

CHAPTER 5

INTRODUCTION TO DIVING TECHNIQUES

Diving is essentially the most important part of the game for a goalkeeper. The goalkeeper must make things look easy, when they're actually really difficult. The right stance of the body, balance, and the right steps before and after a shot are some of the important factors for success.

DRILL 1A DIVING (MEDIUM BALLS) - SITTING POSITION (LEVEL 1)

Description The goalkeeper stands on the ground between two cones 2 meters apart. The assistant is positioned 2-3 meters in front of him. The assistant throws medium height balls to the right and left side of the goalkeeper. The goalkeeper dives for medium height balls and secures the ball in his hands.

Advice (1) Reverse move of the legs. - (2) Correct basic position of the hands that resembles the letter "W". (3) Stability and protection of the ball.

Coaching Points See the coaching points for the next drill (1b).

DRILL 1B — DIVING (MEDIUM BALLS) - KNEELING (LEVEL 1)

Description The goalkeeper kneels on the ground between two cones 2 meters apart. The assistant is positioned 2-3 meters in front of him. The assistant throws medium height balls to the right and left side of the goalkeeper. The goalkeeper dives for medium height balls and secures the ball in his hands.

Advice The same as the previous drill.

Coaching Points

1. Ready hands.
2. React towards the ball and don't fall too soon.
3. Place both hands in front of the body.

INTRODUCTION TO DIVING TECHNIQUES

drill 1b

DRILL 2   FALLS NEAR THE FEET - KNEES (LEVEL 1)

One of the most challenging falls is the one where the ball rolls next to the goalkeeper's feet.

Description The goalkeeper is between two cones (2 m. apart) and on his knees. The assistant stands 2-3 meters in front of him and passes balls to the left and right of the goalkeeper's body. The goalkeeper performs falls with stable grips.

Advice The legs move away and in the opposite direction of the fall. The hands move away from the body and reach out to the ball faster.

Coaching Points
1. See coaching points from previous drill.
2. Position the lower hand backwards so that it is in contact with the ground.
3. Position the second hand on and behind the ball.
4. The lower hand lifts the other hand and stabilizes the ball.
5. Fall gently to the side and on the shoulder.
5. Catch with STABILITY. Pull the ball into the chest area for SECURITY.

INTRODUCTION TO DIVING TECHNIQUES

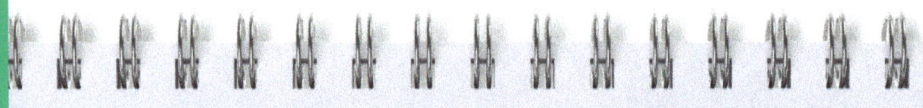

DRILL 3 — MEDIUM HEIGHT FALLS - STANDING POSITION (LEVEL 1)

Description The goalkeeper is in a standing position between two cones (2 meters apart) on his knees. The assistant stands 2-3 meters in front of him and passes medium height balls to the left and to the right of the goalkeeper's body. The goalkeeper performs medium height falls with stable grips.

Advice 1 Effort is made with the leg in the direction of the fall.

Advice 2 Energetic step.

Advice 3 Correct "W" handling technique for the catch.

Advice 4 Sometimes the goalkeeper must take extra steps in order to catch balls further away from his body.

Coaching Points

1. Always be in a state of readiness.
2. React towards the ball. Do not fall too soon.
3. Direct both hands in front of the body.

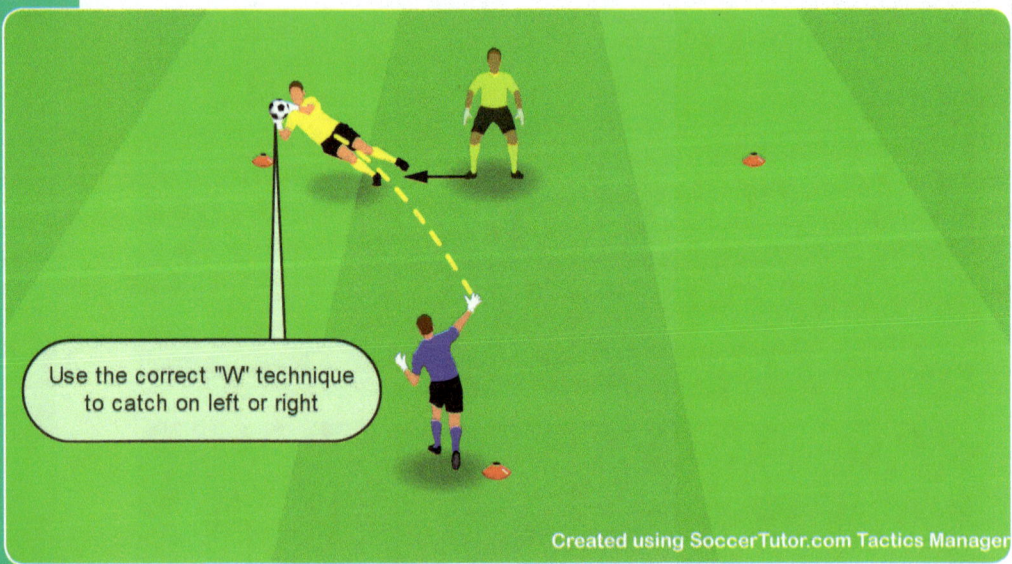

Use the correct "W" technique to catch on left or right

Goalkeepers require many hours of work with small goals to achieve each time. Only then will the correct falling techniques be learned. We train low, medium and high balls both close and far from the body

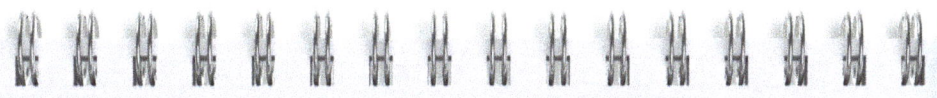

DRILL 4 QUICK REACTIONS TO FIRST TIME SHOT (LEVEL 2)

Description The goalkeeper is in a standing position between two small goals (2 m. x 0,5 m.) with a ball. The assistant stands 5 m. in front of him.

The goalkeeper passes low balls to the assistant who will then shoot first time and try to score a goal. The goalkeeper must react quickly to catch the shot.

Advice 1 Always be in a position of readiness.

Advice 2 Effort is made with the leg in the direction of the fall.

Advice 3 Energetic step.

Advice 4 Correct "W" catch.

Advice 5 Sometimes the goalkeeper must take extra steps in order to catch balls further away from his body.

DRILL 5 — SAVES WITH DIFFERENT CATCHING GRIPS (LEVEL 2)

Description The goalkeeper stands in front of the goal. The assistant stands in the penalty area and moves while holding a ball in his hands.

The assistant strikes the ball towards various points of the goal, forcing the goalkeeper to use the correct grip or fall technique for each instance.

Advice The goalkeeper must align himself with the path of the ball quickly. He must always choose the best reaction.

Coaching Points

1. It is crucial that the goalkeeper understands what he is doing, which grip to use and when.

2. On the occasions that he cannot catch the ball securely, he must parry it safely. This is accomplished by the goalkeeper opening his palm and pushing the ball away and to the side of the goal.

Shots are different angles and heights

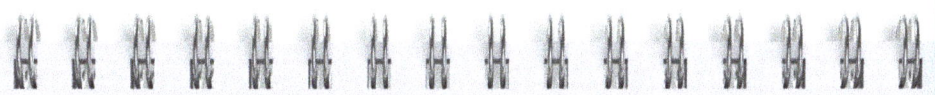

DRILL 6A   QUICK DECISIONS - CATCH OR PARRY (LEVEL 2)

Description The goalkeeper stands in front of the goal. The assistant stands at a 5 m. distance while holding a ball in his hands.

The assistant kicks the ball with controlled force. The goalkeeper must quickly decide if he should catch or parry the ball.

Coaching Points

1. Be in a state of readiness in the initial goalkeeper position.

2. Remain standing for as long as possible.

3. Evaluate the path and height of the ball.

4. Decide when you will catch and when you will parry the ball. Use the most appropriate grip technique.

5. React fast (stand up fast) in order to save a potential second shot.

INTRODUCTION TO DIVING TECHNIQUES

DRILL 6B   PUNCHES OR CHANGE OF PATH (LEVEL 2)

Description The goalkeeper stands in front of the goal. The assistant stands in the penalty area while holding a ball in his hands. The assistant kicks the ball with controlled force in order to score a goal.

In this variation of the previous two drills, the goalkeeper must push (parry with hands) or punch the ball (fists) away from the goal.

The goalkeeper does not catch the ball, but instead focuses on getting the ball as far away from danger as possible.

Coaching Points

1. Be in a state of readiness in the initial goalkeeper position.
2. Remain standing for as long as possible.
3. Evaluate the path and height of the ball.
4. Decide when you will use your fists and when you will parry the ball away from goal.
5. React fast (stand up fast) in order to save a potential second shot.

GK now decides to "Parry" or "Punch"

CHAPTER 6

POSITIONING

The goalkeeper moves in a virtual semi-circle that extends from one goal-post to the other. The position of the goalkeeper should always be between the ball and the center of the goal. The distance between the player that has the ball and the goalkeeper should permit the latter to react while narrowing the angles. If the goalkeeper has the right position, it is highly probable he will emerge victorious.

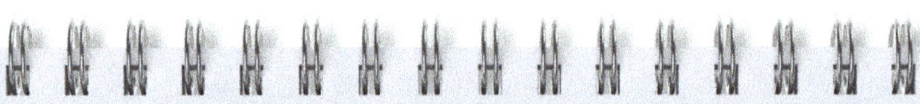

DRILL 1   ARC POSITIONING (LEVEL 1)

Description The goalkeeper stands in front of the goal-posts. From the one goal-post to the other, there are cones in a semi-circle formation. There are balls in different positions 10-15 meters from goal, as shown.

The assistant move towards the balls in order to shoot. The goalkeeper must always take up the right position relative to the ball that the assistant has chosen.

Coaching Points

1. Take the correct steps.
2. Take small steps.
3. Take up the right position.
4. Always be at the virtual line formed by the ball, the goalkeeper and the center of the goal-posts.
5. Ready your stance until the shot.

Coach moves round and can shoot with any ball. GK must react quickly to save.

Created using SoccerTutor.com Tactics Manager

DRILL 2   HANDBALL (LEVEL 1)

Description The goalkeeper stands in front of the goal-posts. There are three assistants, one in the center and the other two at the sides. There is a distance of 10-15 m. between the assistants and the goal.

The assistants throw the ball to each other and expect from the goalkeeper to take up the right position every time. When an assistant wants to shoot, he has to first drop the ball to the ground so it bounces at least once - then he can shoot.

Coaching Points

1. Always expect a shot. Take up the right position quickly.

2, Use the correct steps.

3. Be prepared and be in the right position when the time comes for a shot. Use the proper hand position.

4. React quickly in order to make a second save if necessary.

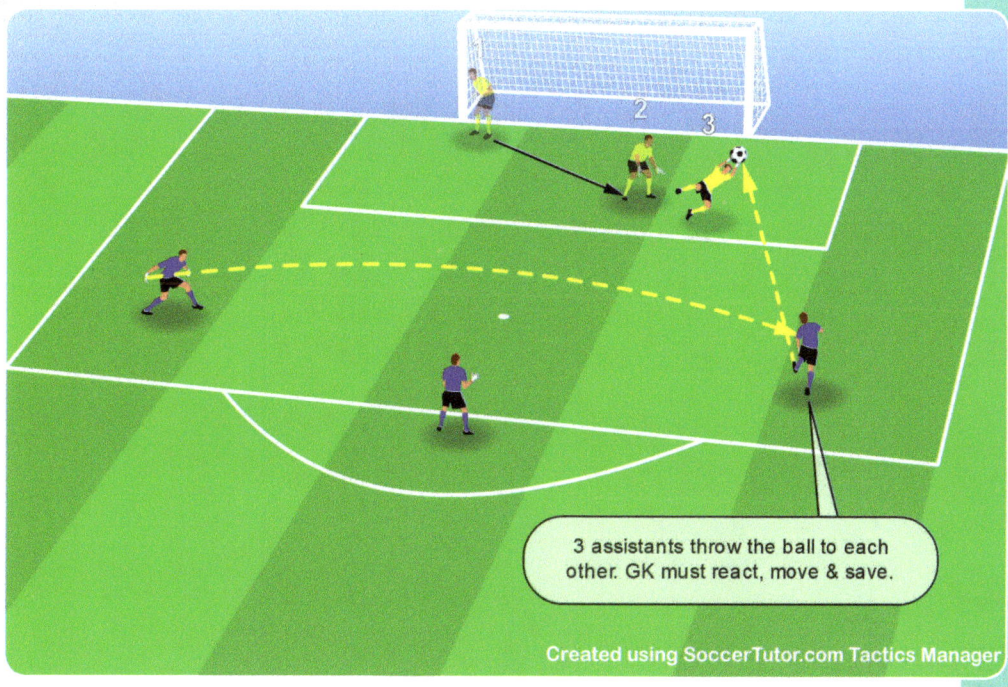

3 assistants throw the ball to each other. GK must react, move & save.

Created using SoccerTutor.com Tactics Manager

F POSITIONING

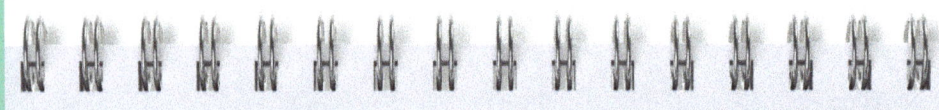

DRILL 3 SHOT FROM AN ANGLE WITH A MOVING PLAYER (LEVEL 1)

Description The goalkeeper stands in front of the goal. The assistant is moving with the ball at his feet at different angles, before deciding when to shoot (at an angle).

The goalkeeper must follow the trajectory of the ball, take up the right positions and always be prepared for a shot.

Coaching Points

1. Always expect a shot.
2. Take up the right position quickly.
3. Use the correct steps.
4. Be prepared and in the right position, when the time comes for the shot.
5. Use the proper hand position and grip technique.
6. React quickly in order to make a second save if necessary.

Assistants dribbles at varying angles & shoots. GK must react, move & save.

Goalkeeper Training Methodology

DRILL 4 — SHOT FROM DIFFERENT ANGLES (LEVEL 2)

Description The goalkeeper stands in front of the goal. There are three assistants; one in the center, one on the right side and one on the left. All of them are positioned outside the penalty area.

The coach calls to each one of the assistants to kick the ball one at a time. The assistant that is called makes an opening with the ball and then takes a shot. The opening is made in order for the goalkeeper to have the chance to position himself correctly.

Once the name has been called, the goalkeeper must move quickly in order to save the incoming shot.

Coaching Points The coaching points are the same as the previous drill.

Assistants take turns to shoot (coach calls one at a time). GK must react, move to new angle & save each shot.

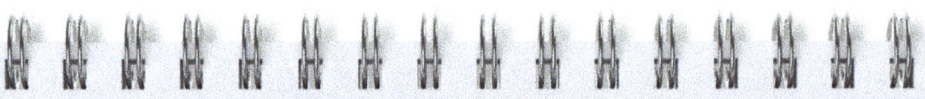

DRILL 5   SHOT AFTER A BOUNCE (LEVEL 2)

Description The goalkeeper stands in front of the goal. In the center and at the edge of the penalty area there are large cones.

The assistant stands behind the cones and holds a ball in his hands. He throws it onto the cones and the ball moves in an unpredictable direction. The assistant then either takes a shot or controls the ball and then takes a shot.

The goalkeeper must wait for the ball to move into its unpredictable path after hitting the cones and then very quickly position himself correctly, in order to have the best possible reaction.

Coaching Points

1. You must have a good initial position and expect a shot at any moment.
2. Cut the diagonals.
3. Take another step forward if the assistant controls the ball before he shoots.
4. Be prepared when he takes the shot.
6. Use the correct grip technique.
7. React quickly in order to make a second save if necessary.

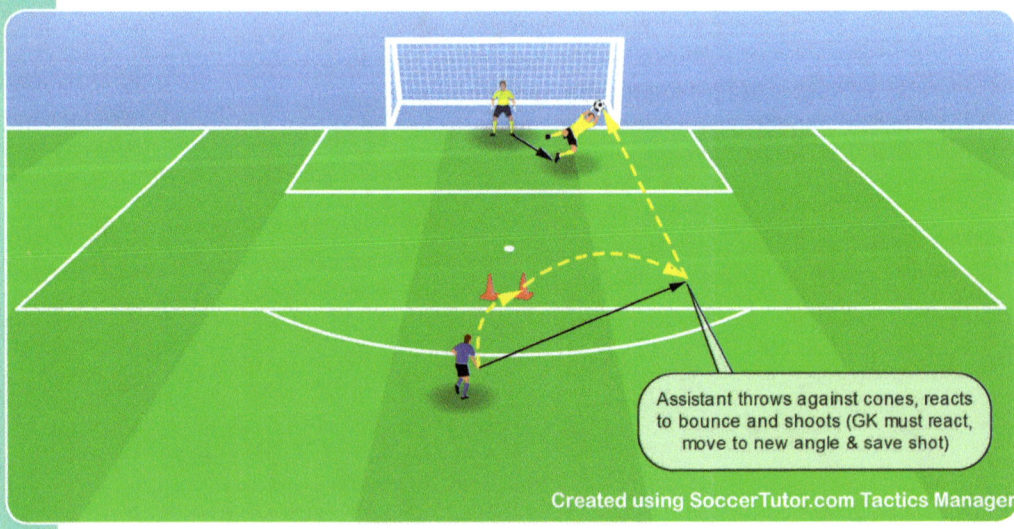

Assistant throws against cones, reacts to bounce and shoots (GK must react, move to new angle & save shot)

Created using SoccerTutor.com Tactics Manager

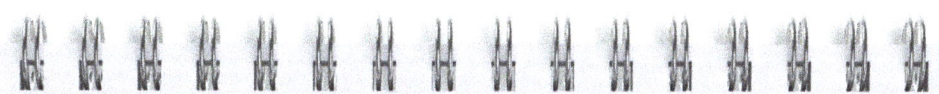

DRILL 6   TURN AND SAVE (LEVEL 2)

Description The goalkeeper stands in front of the goal with his back turned to the pitch. The assistant stands with balls at the edge of the penalty area. Each time he makes a move with the ball at his feet he will order the goalkeeper to turn around.

The goalkeeper will have to determine the position of the ball quickly and position himself correctly for the shot.

Advice This drill tests the adaptability of the goalkeeper to take up the right positions.

Coaching Points

1. Quickly align yourself with the path of the ball.
2. Cut the diagonals.
3. Be prepared when he takes the shot.
4. Use the correct grip technique.
5. React quickly in order to make a second save if necessary.

Assistant moves and shouts for GK to turn around

POSITIONING

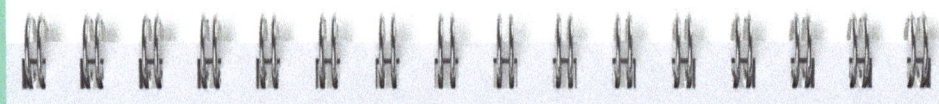

DRILL 7 FOLLOW THE BALL (LEVEL 2)

Description The goalkeeper stands in front of the goal. There are four assistants. Three of them are outside the penalty area (center and side) and the fourth is on the penalty spot with his back to the goal.

One of the three assistants passes the ball to the assistant on the penalty spot and he turns and passes to another assistant. After a small or large number of passes, the assistants will attempt a shot at goal. The goalkeeper must observe the various changes of the path of the ball and always be positioned properly for the shots.

Advice 1 Corrects steps, eyes fixed on the ball at all times, body weight positioned forward.

Advice 2 Make the right decision whether you should catch or parry the ball.

Coaching Points
1. Quickly align yourself with the path of the ball.
2. Cut the diagonals.
3. Be prepared when he takes the shot.
4. Use the correct grip technique.

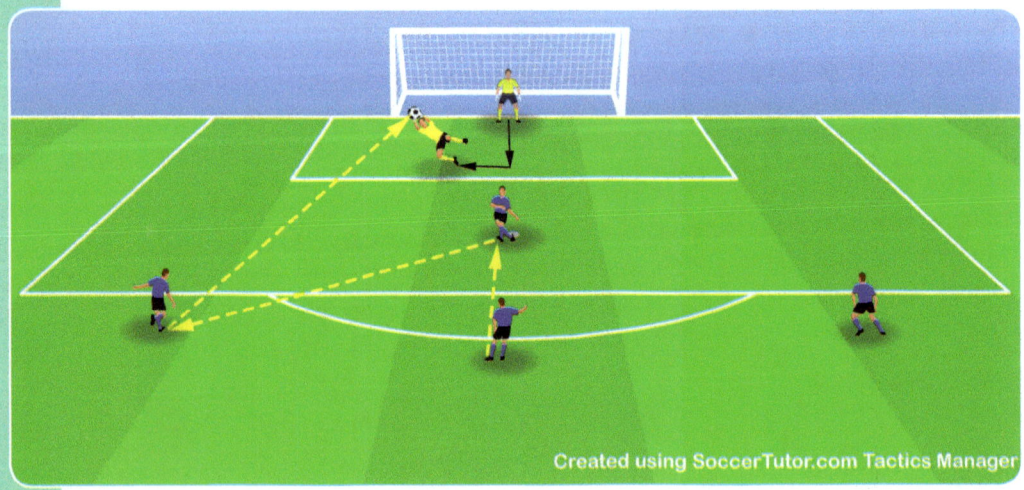

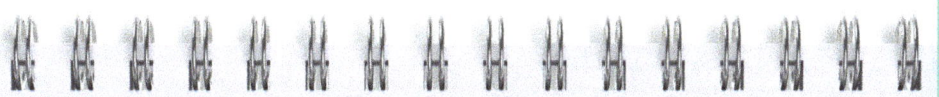

DRILL 8   **MULTIPLE SHOT OPTIONS (LEVEL 2)**

Description The goalkeeper stands in front of the goal. There are three assistants, one in the center, one on the right side and one on the left. All of them are positioned outside the penalty area and all of them have a ball.

The coach stands behind the goalkeeper and indicates to the assistants which one will take a shot.

The assistant first takes a touch of the ball and then takes a shot. The goalkeeper must react between the various shots quickly and with the best possible positioning.

Coaching Points The same as the previous drill.

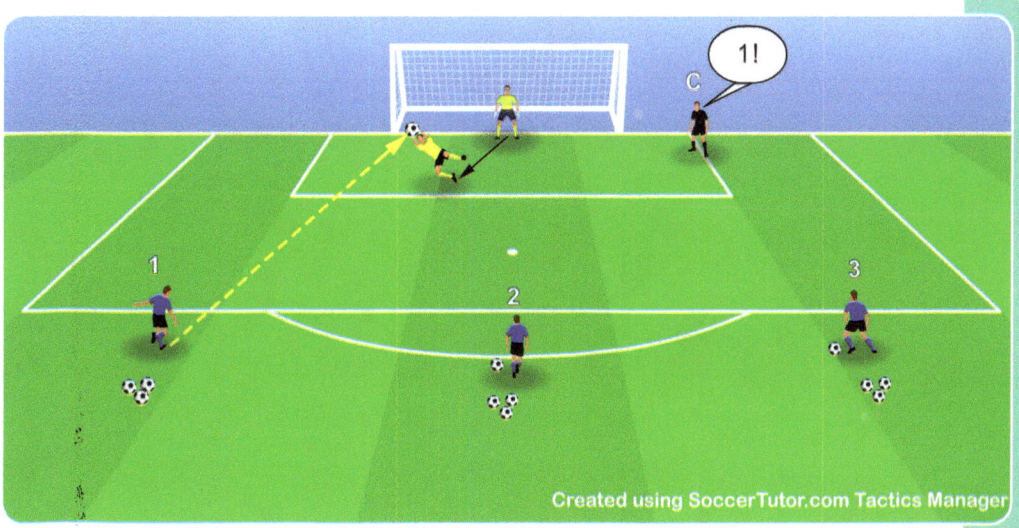

CHAPTER 7

SAVING ON THE MOVE

Occasionally, the goalkeeper is obliged to deflect the ball while he is in motion. In order to achieve this, he must have perfect coordination, excellent spatial awareness and time perception.

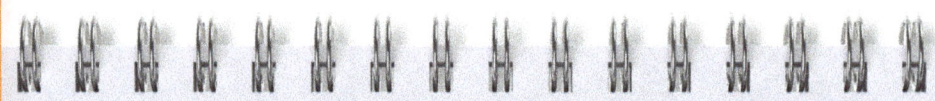

DRILL 1   ZIG-ZAG DRILL – DIVING (LEVEL 2)

Description The goalkeeper stands in front of the goal. There are cones in front of him in a diagonal formation. The assistant stands at the edge of the ox with balls. The goalkeeper moves diagonal through the cones (zig-zag). At the end, the assistant shoots and the goalkeeper must try to save the shot.

Advice 1 Small steps, lateral movement, stable core. The goalkeeper must be ready for the shot when he comes out of the cones.

Advice 2 In order to raise the level of difficulty, the assistant may shoot whenever he wants, without the goalkeeper having to finish the zig-zag through the cones first. The goalkeeper must therefore be ready the whole time.

Coaching Points
1. Move quickly and with rhythm.
2. Your hands should be steady and ready.
3. Keep your head steady.
4. Use the proper hand position.

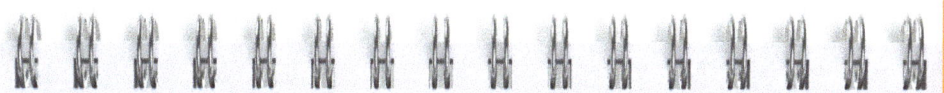

DRILL 2 — DIVING IN A TRIANGLE FORMATION (LEVEL 2)

Description We create a triangle using cones 5 meters apart. On every side of the triangle, there's an assistant with a ball.

The goalkeeper moves across the different sides of the triangle, diving when needed to react to the different shots.

Advice 1 Move around the triangle 2 times (6 total shots) and then rest. Small steps.

Advice 2 Accelerate and decelerate during movement.

Coaching Points

1, Move your legs quickly between the sides.
2, Spread your feet shoulder-width apart.
3. Keep your hands steady during movement.
4. Keep your head steady.
5. Right decision whether you should catch or deflect the ball.

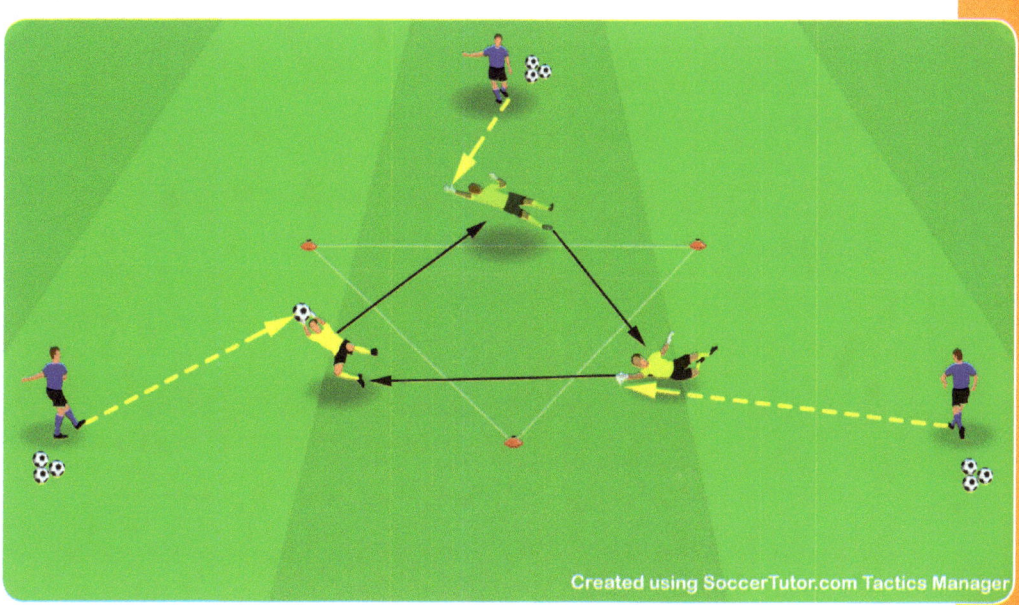

SAVING ON THE MOVE

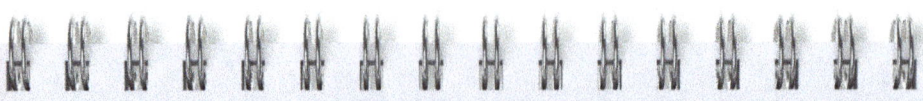

DRILL 3   FALL WITH FORWARD MOTION (LEVEL 2)

There are a number of circumstances in which the goalkeeper must react while he is in motion. This drill prepares the goalkeeper to react while he is in a forward motion.

Description The goalkeeper is in goal and moves towards the assistant who is positioned outside of the penalty area with balls.

The assistant can pass or take short or long shots while the goalkeeper is in motion.

Advice 1 Take fast and short steps. Position the body quickly in alignment with the ball.

Coaching Points

1. Keep your head steady.
2. Stay calm and prepare to clear the ball.

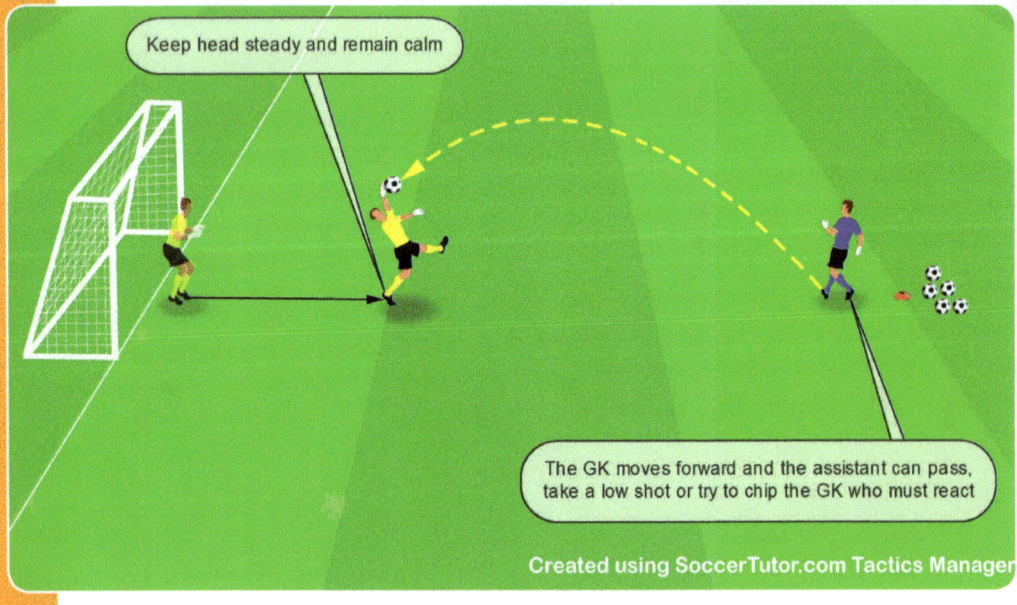

DRILL 4A FALL BACK IN MOTION (LEVEL 2)

In this drill, the layout consists of a goal and two cones 7-8 meters out that are aligned with the goal-posts.

Description The goalkeeper stands next to one of the cones. The assistant stands outside of the penalty area with balls (in alignment with the center of the goal). The goalkeeper takes steps backwards and responds to shots made by the assistant. He then repeats the drill, changes his starting position to the other side.

Coaching Points

1. Take quick cross-steps towards the center of the goal and in alignment with the path of the ball.
2. Keep your head steady.
3. Try to be in a state of readiness and keep your body weight forward.
4. Use the appropriate grip technique.

DRILL 4B FALLS WITH BACKWARD MOTION (LEVEL 2)

In this drill we have a goal and three cones in the positions shown. The two side cones are aligned with the posts and the third one is in the center.

Description The goalkeeper starts next to one of the side cones. The assistant stands outside of the penalty area with balls (in alignment with the center of the goal). Starting from one of the side cones, the goalkeeper takes steps backwards and responds to shots made by the assistant. He then takes steps from the central cone and finally from the other side cone.

Coaching Points
1. Take quick cross-steps towards the center of the goal and in alignment with the path of the ball.
2. Keep your head steady.
3. Try to be in a state of readiness and keep your body weight forward.
4. Use the appropriate grip technique.

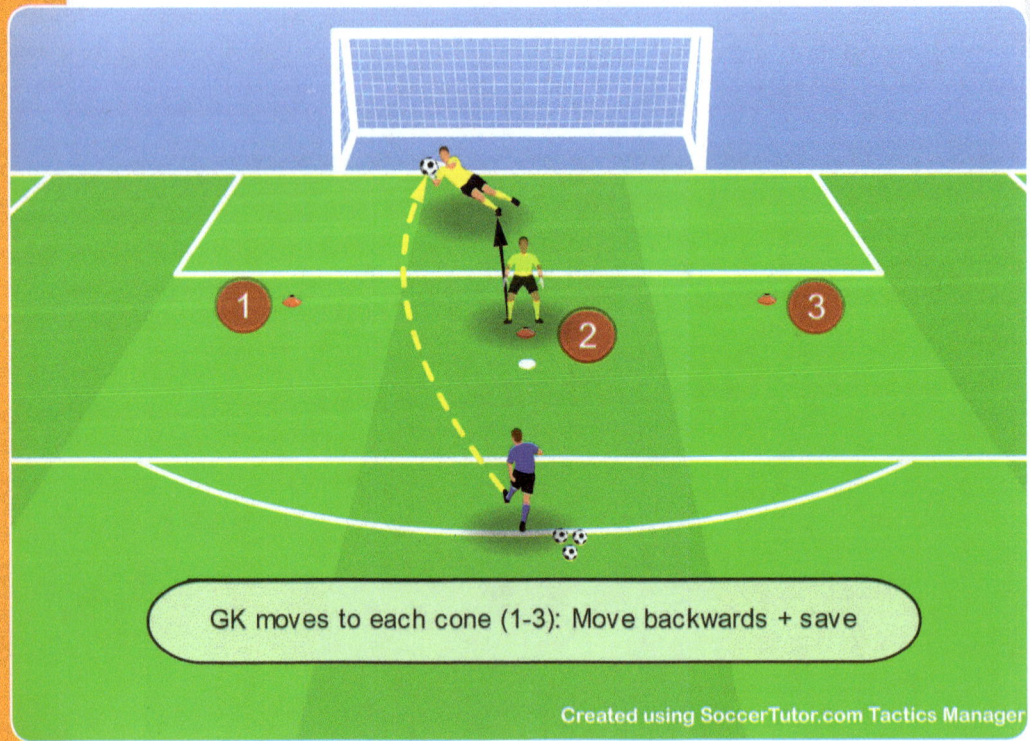

GK moves to each cone (1-3): Move backwards + save

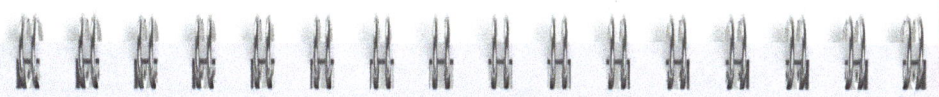

DRILL 5   FALLS WITH SIDEWAYS MOTION (LEVEL 2)

Description The goalkeeper stands in the center of the goal. Two assistants stand to the side of the posts with balls. One assistant gives a verbal signal to the goalkeeper and then takes a shot. The goalkeeper has to run towards the post to clear the ball.

Advice 1 The points of departure may vary.

Advice 2 We can position an assistant in the center of the 6-yard box to follow up and score if the goalkeeper makes any unstable clearances.

Coaching Points
1. The coaching points from the previous drill still apply.
2. Keep your feet apart at shoulder width.
3. Decelerate in order to have the best reaction to the shot.
4. If you have the time, align with the path of the ball.
5. Choose if you are going to catch or clear the ball.
6. Be prepared to clear the ball with your feet.

CHAPTER 8

AN IMPERFECT WORLD

This chapter investigates the variable elements that a goalkeeper may be confronted with during the path of a game. The weather, the condition of the field, even his own teammates! The goalkeeper may not always have the time to prepare his body for the ideal "starting position". Regardless of this, he must always be prepared to react to any shot, at any moment and under the most extreme and bizarre circumstances.

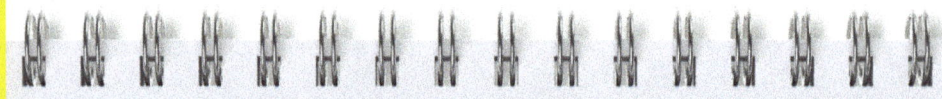

DRILL 1   **FLIP AND CLEAR (LEVEL 2)**

Description The goalkeeper stands in the middle of the goal. The assistant stands 5-6 meters away,

The goalkeeper performs a forward role (flips over) and as he rises, the assistant shoots at goal towards him.

Advice When we flip on the ground, we allow our body to roll forward. Hands should be placed ahead for support.

Coaching Points

1. Keep your head steady.
2. Be in a state of readiness with your body weight placed forward.
3. Decide whether you will catch or clear the ball.
4. Use the correct grip technique.
5. Be prepared to clear the ball with any part of your body.

120   Goalkeeper Training Methodology

DRILL 2 — CLEAR FROM A SITTING POSITION (LEVEL 2)

Description The goalkeeper is in a sitting position in the middle of the goal. When he receives a verbal signal from the assistant (who is 5 meters away with a ball), he stands up quickly and reacts to a long shot.

Advice Use both your hands to rise while pushing your body forward. Use both feet as a base to lift your body into an alert position.

Coaching Points
1. The coaching points from the previous drill still apply.
2. Stand up as quickly as possible.
3. Keep your legs apart at shoulder width.
4. React quickly in order to be able to make a second save.

drill 2

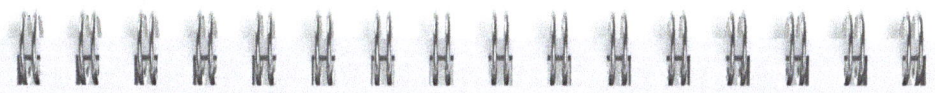

DRILL 3   CLEAR FROM A SITTING POSITION & BACKWARD SHIFT (LEVEL 2)

Description The goalkeeper is in a sitting position, approximately 1 meter outside of the 6-yard box.

When he receives a verbal signal from the assistant (who is standing outside the penalty area with balls), he stands up quickly and with backward diagonal steps, he attempts to prevent a goal being scored (catch or parry/punch). The assistant attempts to pass the balls over the goalkeeper and score.

Advice Always take criss-cross steps.

Coaching Points
1. Stand up as quickly as possible.
2. Take fast and small steps.
3. Keep your head steady.
4. Eyes must be fixed on the ball at all times.
5. Align yourself with the path of the ball.
6. Decide whether you will catch or clear the ball.
7. Use the correct grip technique.

drill 3

2

3

4

124 Goalkeeper Training Methodology

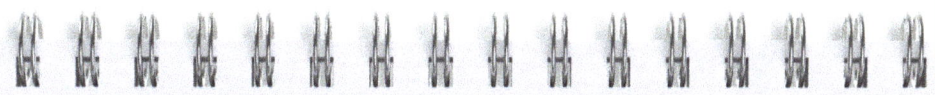

DRILL 4   **CLEAR FROM A STANDING POSITION & SIDEWAYS SHIFT (LEVEL 2)**

Description The goalkeeper stands beside the post in a state of readiness facing the corner arc. When he receives a verbal signal from the assistant (who is standing near the edge of the penalty area with balls), he turns quickly and with fast steps towards the direction of the ball, he attempts to catch or clear it.

The assistant waits for the goalkeeper to take steps and then tries to kick the ball into the exposed part of the goal.

Advice Criss-cross and straight steps should be taken, depending on the distance and location of the ball. Move at maximum speed.

Coaching Points

1. Determine the location of the ball as quickly as possible.
2. Align yourself with the path of the ball.
3. Take fast and small steps.
4. Keep your head steady with fixed on the ball.
5. Decide whether you will catch or clear the ball.

Align yourself with the ball with eyes fixed. Take short, fast steps to move & save.

AN IMPERFECT WORLD

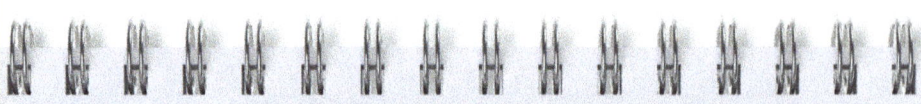

DRILL 5   CLEAR FROM GROUND POSITIONS (LEVEL 2)

Description The goalkeeper stands beside the post, face down and facing the corner arc. When he receives a verbal signal from the assistant, he stands up quickly and turns to defend the exposed part of the goal from the assistant's shot. He must take fast steps towards the direction of the ball and attempt to clear or catch it. The assistant waits for the goalkeeper to take steps and then kicks the ball towards the opposite direction.

Advice 1 We repeat the drill with variations of the goalkeeper's position (e.g. on his back, on his knees etc.). The assistant can raise the level of difficulty by taking shots from different positions.

Advice 2 The goalkeeper can have many starting points in the wide areas and not just by the goal-posts.

Coaching Points

1. Determine the location of the ball and stand up as quickly as possible.
2. Align yourself with the path of the ball.
3. Take fast and small steps. Keep your head steady.
4. Eyes must be fixed on the ball at all times.

1. Lie down facing out
2. Stand up and move across
3. Save the shot towards the other side

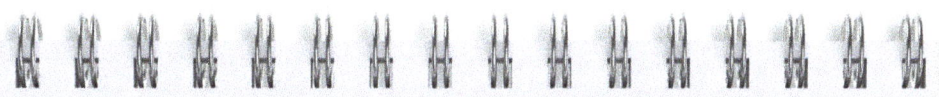

DRILL 6A   CHANGING PATH OF BALL WITH CONES (LEVEL 2)

Description The goalkeeper stands in the middle of the goal. Two cones (or other obstacles that can change the path of the ball) are placed 2-3 meters in front of him. The assistant stands at the edge of the penalty area with balls that he kicks towards the cones in order for the path of the ball to be disrupted and the goalkeeper to be forced into instinctive reactions.

Advice Even if the ball does not hit one of the cones the drill continues normally. The cones represent the players that could be in front of the goalkeeper.

Coaching Points
1. Correct starting position.
2. Do not stand too close to the cones because you will have less time to react.
3. Keep your head steady.
4. Do not panic if you momentarily lose sight of the ball.
5. Follow the path of the ball but be prepared for a change of path if the ball hits the cones.
6. React quickly in order to be able to make a second save if necessary.

AN IMPERFECT WORLD

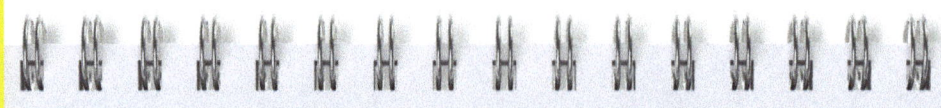

DRILL 6B   CHANGING PATH OF BALL WITH CONES (LEVEL 2)

Description The goalkeeper stands in the middle of the goal. Three cones are in the positions shown and they are wider apart than they were in the previous drill.

The assistant stands on the edge of the penalty area with balls that he kicks towards the cones in order for the path of the balls to be disrupted and the goalkeeper to be forced into instinctive reactions.

Advice Even if the ball does not hit one of the cones, the goalkeeper is in a very challenging and high-pressure situation.

Coaching Points The same as the previous drill.

DRILL 7   CHANGING PATH OF BALL WITH PLAYER (LEVEL 3)

This drill is similar to the previous one, but instead of cones we use one or two players or assistants. These players serve the purpose of creating visual obstruction and physical diversions/deflections of the ball.

Description The goalkeeper stands in the middle of the goal. One or two players stand in front of him at a 5-6 meter distance.

The player or assistant stands on the edge of the penalty area with balls that he kicks towards the goal.

Coaching Points The same as the previous two drills.

GK must react to deflections off assistant

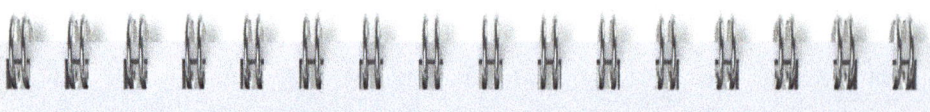

DRILL 8A   LONG DISTANCE SHOTS (LEVEL 1)

Sometimes long shots can cause many problems because the ball travels in the air for a long time. The basic rule for reacting to long shots is to align ourselves with the ball and remain calm when the ball changes its path at the last second.

Description The goalkeeper stands in the middle of the goal. The assistant stands 5-10 meters outside the penalty area with balls. He takes shots (low shots, long shots etc.) while constantly changing positions.

Coaching Points
1. Correct starting position.
2. Quickly align yourself with the path of the ball.
3. Decide whether you will catch or clear the ball.
4. Use the correct grip technique.
5. React quickly in order to be able to make a second save if necessary.

Remain calm, take small steps & keep head steady

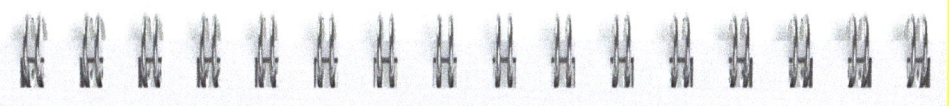

DRILL 8B **LONG DISTANCE SHOTS (LEVEL 2)**

Description The goalkeeper stands in the middle of the goal.

Two assistants stand 2-3 meters outside the penalty area at diagonal angles with balls. They take turns taking a variety of shots (low shots, long shots etc.).

Coaching Points The same as the previous drill.

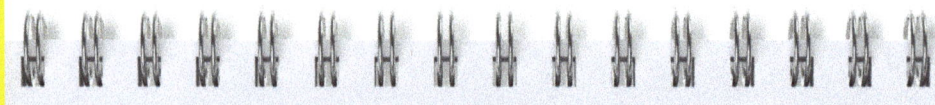

DRILL 9 SAVES USING THE FEET (LEVEL 1)

Drills in which the goalkeeper saves with the use of his feet are acceptable and will be useful many times in a game.

Description The goalkeeper stands in the middle of the goal. Many balls are aligned along the six-yard line.

Two assistants take turns at kicking hard shots close to the goalkeeper's body. The goalkeeper must turn the balls away with the use of his feet.

Advice Turn the ball away with the inside of the foot. Try to turn the ball away sideways, away from the goal.

Coaching Points

1, Correct starting position.
2. Remain calm.
3. Take many small steps.
4. Keep your head steady.

Use inside of the foot to save and clear the ball sideways away from goal

Goalkeeper Training Methodology

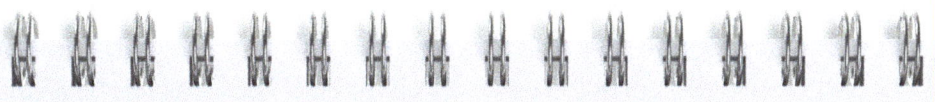

DRILL 10 — SAVES USING THE FEET AND HANDS (LEVEL 2)

Description The goalkeeper stands in the middle of the goal. Many balls are aligned along the six-yard line.

Two assistants take turns at kicking low or medium height shots, always at or close to the goalkeeper's body.

Advice The goalkeeper must decide if he is going to use his feet or his hands.

Coaching Points

1. Correct starting position.
2. Remain calm.
3. Take many small steps.
4. Keep your head steady.
5. Decide whether you will catch or clear the ball.
6. Turn the ball away sideways, away from the goal.

Asssistants can test the GK with continuous low or medium height shots

AN IMPERFECT WORLD

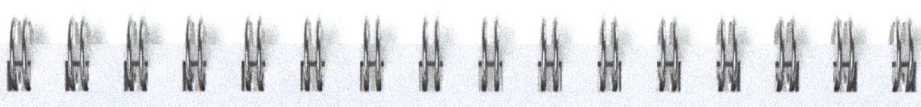

DRILL 11   SUDDEN SHOT (LEVEL 1)

Description The assistant stands outside the box to one side. A cone is placed in line with the center of the goal and on the edge of the penalty area. The assistant runs with the ball past the cone. As soon as he passes the cone, he shoots towards the goal.

The goalkeeper must observe the entire path of the assistant's run and react to the shot. The drill is repeated in both directions.

Advice The more experienced the goalkeeper, the more challenging the shot should be.

Coaching Points

1. Correct starting position.
2. Take many small steps and keep your head steady.
3. Quickly align yourself with the path of the ball.
4. Decide whether you will catch or clear the ball.
5. Use the correct grip technique.
6. React quickly in order to be able to make a second save if necessary.

DRILL 12   SECOND SAVE (LEVEL 2)

There are instances where the goalkeeper cannot clear the ball with one attempt. That is exactly the moment when the goalkeeper must react correctly in order to secure a second chance.

The goalkeeper must get up very quickly after a fall to the ground in order to have a second chance. Second chances are easier to achieve when the body weight is placed forward.

Description The goalkeeper is face down and parallel to the goal line. With a vocal signal from the assistant, he stands up quickly to react to a shot. The attempt is made in the same direction as the goalkeeper is moving.

Advice We progressively change the starting position to cover all variables.

Coaching Points

1. Lift yourself from the ground quickly.
2. Take many small steps and keep your head steady.
3. Decide whether you will catch or clear the ball.

CHAPTER 9

ONE ON ONES

A "one on one" situation demands the correct decision making and courage.

There are three stages in "one on one" contacts:

- Evaluation.
- Correct decision-making.
- Correct technique.

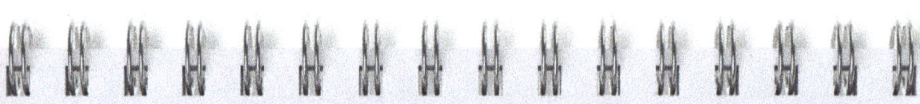

DRILL 1   DROP FROM YOUR KNEES AT AN ANGLE (LEVEL 1)

This drill is for beginner goalkeepers. Working from the knees builds their confidence.

Description The goalkeeper is on his knees (image 1) between two cones (2 meter goal).

The assistant guides the ball towards the goalkeeper from a slight angle. The goalkeeper drops to the assistant's feet and blocks the ball (images 2-4).

Coaching Points

1. Synchronize yourself with the ball.
2. Drop towards the ball. Using both hands, block the ball and secure it to your chest.
3. Protect the ball by closing your legs and head around it.
4. Keep your head steady and your eyes open.

2

3

4

drill 1

ONE ON ONES

139

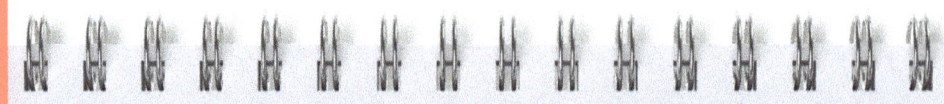

DRILL 2 — DROP FROM SQUATTING POSITION (LEVEL 1)

Description The goalkeeper is in a deep squatting position between two cones (2 meter goal).

The assistant guides the ball towards the goalkeeper from a slight angle (image 2). The goalkeeper drops to the assistant's feet and blocks the ball (images 3-5).

Coaching Points

1. Synchronize yourself with the ball.
2. Grasp the ball and not the player.
3. Drop towards the ball.
4. Extend your arms towards the ball.
5. Using both hands, block the ball and secure it to your chest.
6. Protect the ball by closing your legs and head around it.
7. Keep your head steady and your eyes open.

1

Goalkeeper Training Methodology

drill 2

2

3

4

5

ONE ON ONES

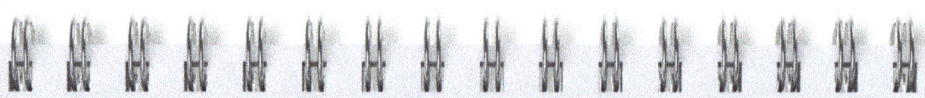

DRILL 3 — DROP TO YOUR KNEES STRAIGHT ON (LEVEL 1)

Description The goalkeeper is on his knees (image 1) between two cones (2 meter goal).

The assistant guides the ball towards the goalkeeper (straight line). The goalkeeper drops to the assistant's feet and blocks the ball.

Coaching Points

1. Synchronize yourself with the ball.
2. Grasp the ball and not the player.
3. Drop towards the ball.
4. Extend your arms towards the ball.
5. Using both hands, block the ball and secure it to your chest.
6. Protect the ball by closing your legs and head around it.
7. Keep your head steady and your eyes open.

1

2

3

4

drill 3

ONE ON ONES

143

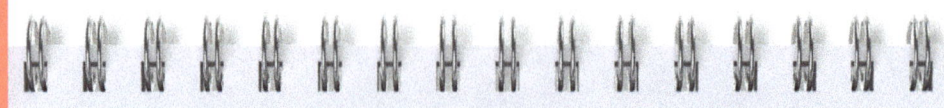

DRILL 4   2 V 1 DROP TO YOUR FEET GAME (LEVEL 2)

Description The goalkeeper and two assistants stand in a 5 m x 5 m square space. Within this square, the goalkeeper and the assistants play a game in which the goalkeeper tries to steal the ball from the assistants.

The assistants move freely within the square and pass to each other - each must try to have at least one touch of the ball.

After 5 successful passes from the assistants, the goalkeeper must rest because it is a highly demanding drill.

Coaching Points
1. Stay still until the ball moves. Bend your knees in a low starting position.
2. Take small steps. Synchronize yourself with the ball.
3. Place pressure on the ball, not the player.
4. Drop towards the ball. Extend your arms towards the ball.
5. Try to block the ball or change its path with any part of the body. Keep your head steady and your eyes open.
6. Bring the ball carrier into a difficult position e.g. close him off in the corner.
7. When the goalkeeper drops, he should extend his arms since they are the longest part of his body.

Goalkeeper Training Methodology

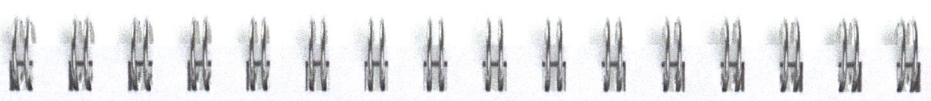

DRILL 5   1 V 1 SITUATION (LEVEL 2)

Description Mark out a 10 m x 6 m space with two small goals at each end.

One goal is the home base for the goalkeeper and the other is the base for the assistant.

The goalkeeper serves a ball to the assistant either with his hands or his feet.

The assistant receives the ball and immediately dribbles towards the goalkeeper's goal in order to take the ball around him and score.

The goalkeeper confronts the assistant as soon as he makes his first touch. His task is to cut him off and take control of the ball or clear it from the area.

Advice Create an impervious wall with your body.

Coaching Points

1. The same as the previous drill.
2. Try to bring the ball carrier into a difficult position e.g. close him off on the sides.

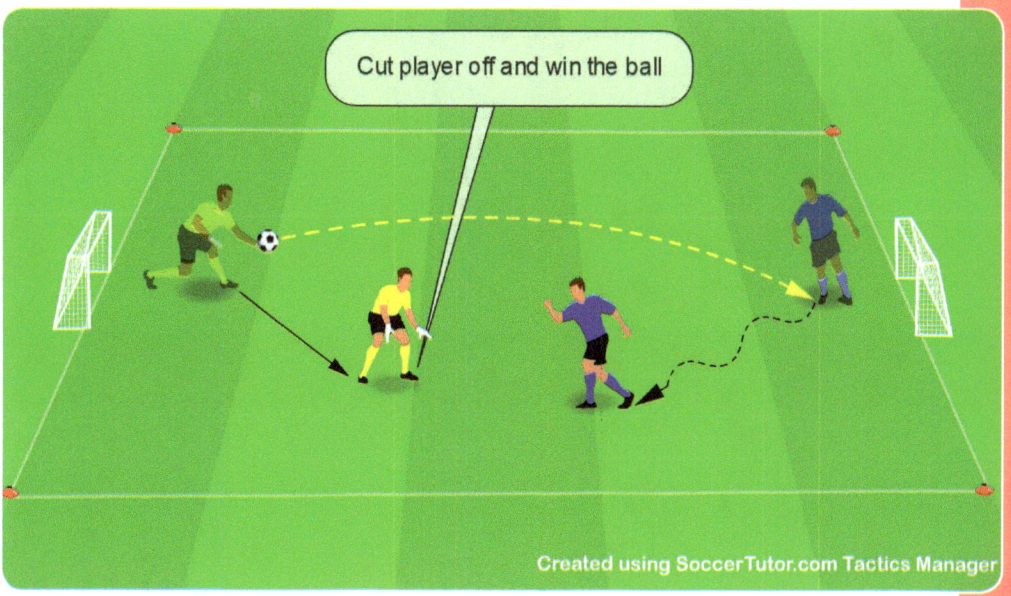

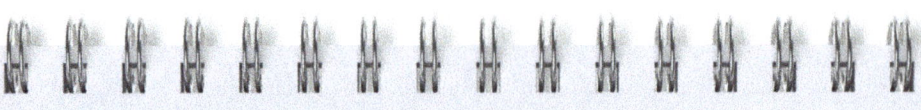

DRILL 6A 1 V 1 GAME (LEVEL 2)

Description Mark out a 10 m x 6 m space with two small goals at each end. The one goal is the home base for one goalkeeper and the other is the home base of the second goalkeeper.

The goalkeeper serves a ball either with his hands or his feet.

The second goalkeeper receives the ball and immediately guides it towards the first goalkeeper's goal in order to beat him and score.

The two goalkeepers work in rotation.

The goalkeeper who serves the ball must wait for the second goalkeeper to take the first touch. He will then run to confront him. His task is to cut him off and take the ball or clear it from the area.

Advice Create an impervious wall with your body.

Coaching Points

1. The same as the previous drill.
2. The prepared to clear the ball with your feet if it is necessary.

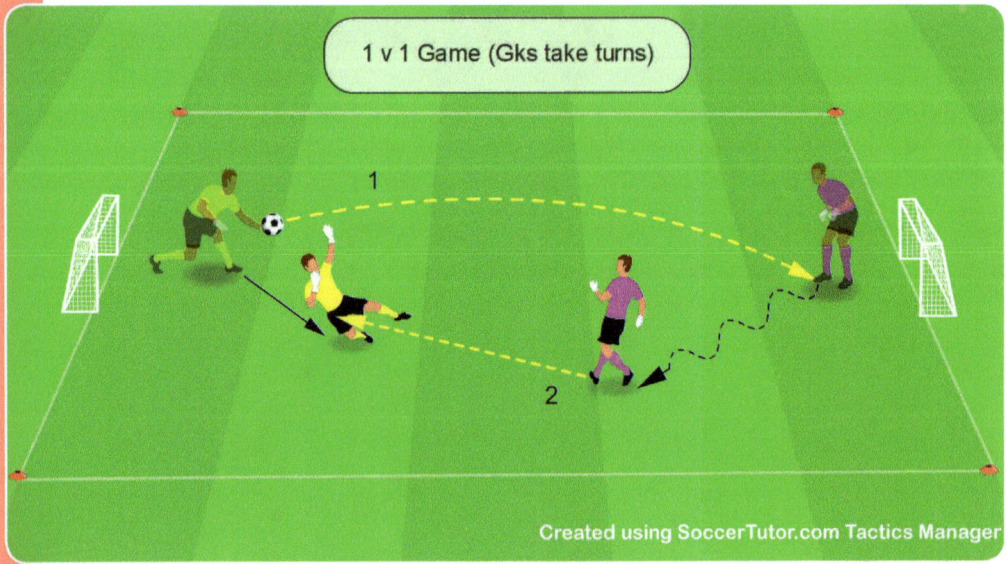

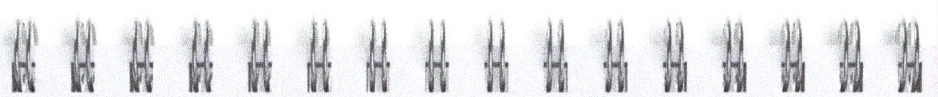

DRILL 6B 1 V 1 FROM THE CENTER GAME (LEVEL 2)

Description Define a 10 m x 6 m space with two medium size goals at each end (not small goals as in the previous drills).

The goalkeeper serves a ball either with his hands or his feet.

The second goalkeeper receives the ball and immediately dribbles towards the first goalkeeper's goal in order to beat him and score.

As soon as his attempt is completed, the drill is repeated by the other goalkeeper.

Advice Create an impervious wall with your body.

Coaching Points

The same as the previous drill.

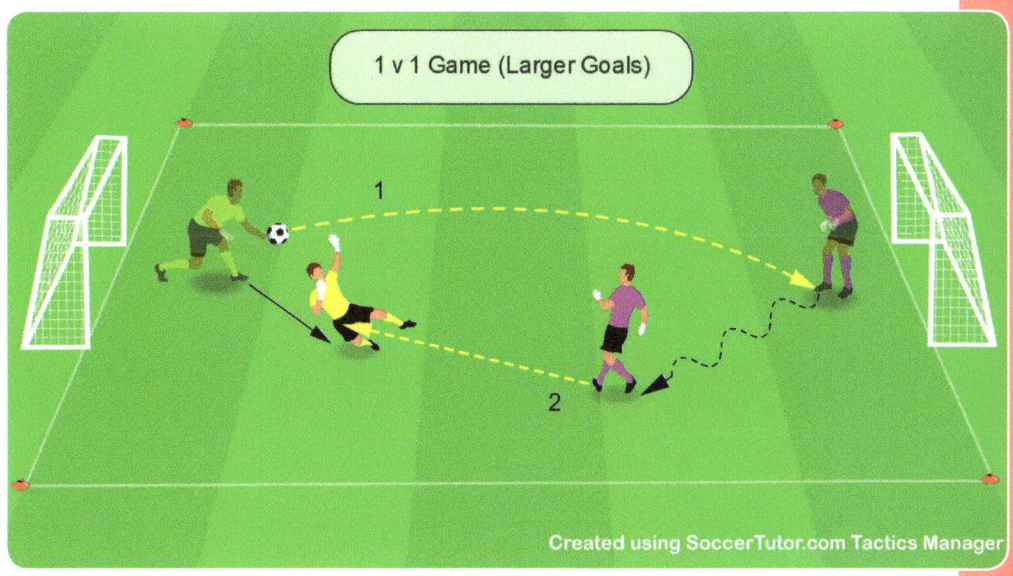

1 v 1 Game (Larger Goals)

ONE ON ONES

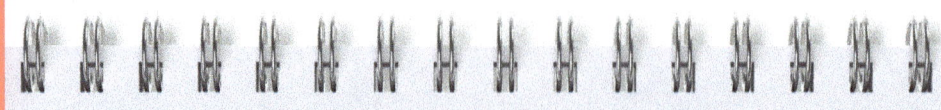

DRILL 6C 1 V 1 FROM THE SIDE GAME (LEVEL 2)

Description Define a 10 m x 6 m space with two medium size goals at each end.

The goalkeeper serves a ball either with his hands or his feet.

The second goalkeeper who receives the ball stands at one of the two corners of the goal. This position is meant to improve the adaptability of the goalkeeper's techniques at various angles in a "one on one" situation.

Once the second goalkeeper receives the ball, he dribbles towards the first goalkeeper to score.

As soon as his attempt is completed, the drill is repeated by the other goalkeeper.

Advice Create an impervious wall with your body.

Coaching Points
The same as the previous drill.

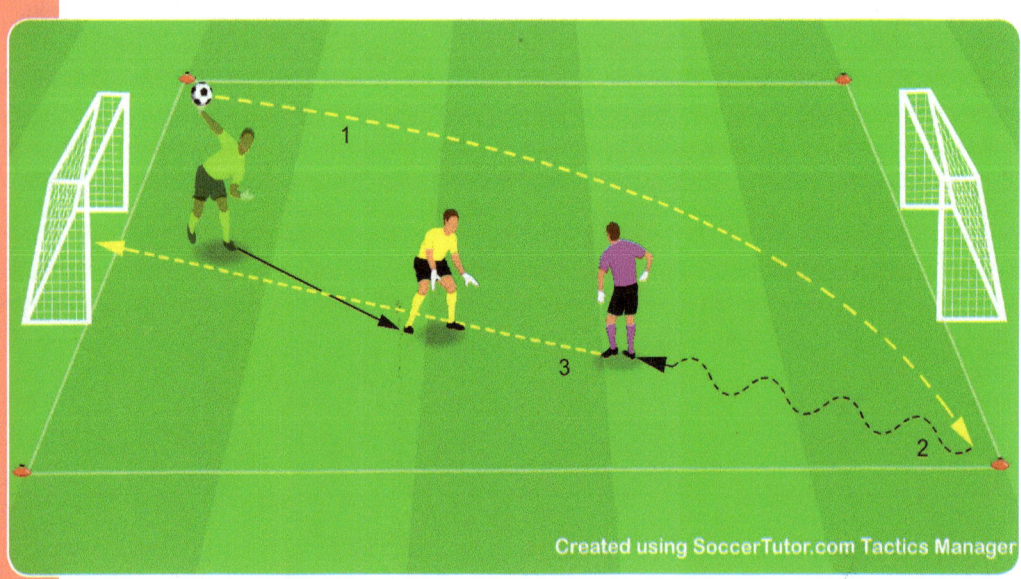

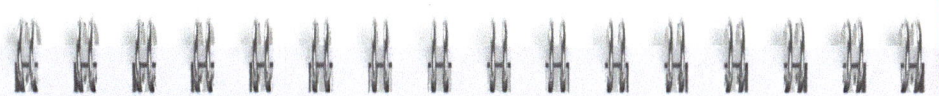

DRILL 7   IMPERVIOUS WALL (LEVEL 2)

Description The goalkeeper is in the goal. There are three balls positioned along the 6-yard box as shown.

The assistant indicates which ball he will take a shot with. The goalkeeper moves towards this ball with the intention of clearing it with any part of his body.

Advice Create an impervious wall with your body.

Coaching Points

1. Extend your body in order to cover the goal as much as possible.
2. Keep your head steady.
3. Be prepared to clear a second time if it is necessary.

Assitant calls out ball + sprints towards it. GK must react and clear the ball.

DRILL 8   1 V 1 - THE RISK TAKER (LEVEL 2)

Description The goalkeeper is in the goal. There are three assistants in front of him level with the penalty spot. One is positioned in the center with balls and two are at the sides within 1-1.5 meters. The central assistant serves balls to the two side assistants who takes turns to attempt to score. The goalkeeper reacts with fast steps towards the attacking player and must make quick and intelligent decisions as to whether he will block, or extend his body like a wall between the ball and the goal.

Advice (1) Run very fast. - (2) Do not lose sight of the ball. - (3) Create an impervious wall with your body.

Coaching Points
1. Move swiftly towards the ball and decide whether you will stay or block.
2. If you decide to stay and extend yourself towards the ball, then begin to do so with your arms.
3. Keep your head steady and your eyes open.
4. Maximize your size by extending your body to cover the goal like a wall.
5. Be prepared to clear the ball a second time if it is necessary.

Assistant serves to left or right. GK must react quickly to save shot.

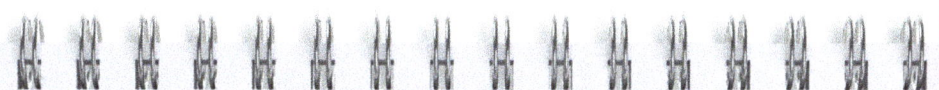

DRILL 9   1 V 1 - CHANGE OF PATH (LEVEL 2)

Description The goalkeeper is on the post facing out diagonally. One of the assistants stands at the side of the 6-yard box with balls (across from the goalkeeper). The second assistant stands in the center and slightly towards the side of the goalkeeper. The first assistant passes balls to the second assistant who attempts to score (he must first take at least one touch before shooting). The goalkeeper shifts parallel to the path of the ball and tries to clear or block the shot by dropping to the attacking player's feet or by blocking the path of the ball.

Advice (1) Run very fast. - (2) Do not lose sight of the ball. - (3) Create an impervious wall with your body.

Coaching Points

1. Decide whether you want to play the ball or change its path.
2. If you decide to move towards the ball, then begin to do so with your hands first.
3. Extend yourself towards the ball, then begin to do so with your arms.
4. Maximize your size by extending your body to cover the goal like a wall.
5. Keep your head steady and your eyes open.
6. Be prepared to clear a second time if it is necessary.

ONE ON ONES

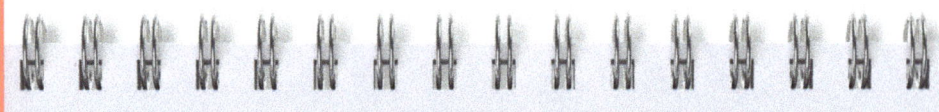

DRILL 10 1 V 1 IN THE PENALTY AREA (LEVEL 3)

Description The goalkeeper is in the goal. An assistant plays the role of the attacking player and runs with the ball towards the goal from outside the penalty area. A second assistant plays the role of the defender and runs to assist the goalkeeper. The goalkeeper runs to close off the attacking player and prevent the goal.

Advice 1 Create an impervious wall with your body.

Advice 2 Buy time by holding off the attacking player until the defender arrives for assistance.

Coaching Points

1. Stay still until the ball moves. Bend your knees in a low starting position.
2. Take small steps. Synchronize yourself with the ball.
3. Put pressure on the ball, not the player.
4. Try to bring the ball carrier into a difficult position at the side of the goal.
5. Be prepared to clear the ball with your feet if it is necessary.

DRILL 11   1 V 1 - CLAIMABLE BALL (LEVEL 3)

Description The goalkeeper is in the goal. An assistant plays the role of the attacking player and another plays the role of a defender - they are positioned approximately 2 meters outside the penalty area. A third assistant is approximately 6 meters outside the penalty area with balls. The third assistant serves claimable balls into the penalty area. The attacker runs and attempts to score with single or multiple touches. The defender tries to intercept the ball and the goalkeeper must react in the best possible way in each circumstance.

Advice This drill is aimed at helping the goalkeeper make correct decisions as to when he should extend towards the ball, when he should stay still and generally acquire training with a large range of different situations.

Coaching Points
1. Stay still until the ball moves. Take small steps.
2. Decide as to whether you should move or remain alert in the starting position.
3. Close in to the direction of the ball. Keep your head steady and your eyes open.
4. Be prepared to clear the ball with your feet if it is necessary.

CHAPTER 10

REACTIONS

Good reaction saves are the result of good technique, physical abilities and improvisation. The correct technique provides you with the possibility of moving towards the right point at the right time. Improvisation is important, since the reaction time isn't long. This chapter will present some situations where the goalkeeper must react swiftly and effectively.

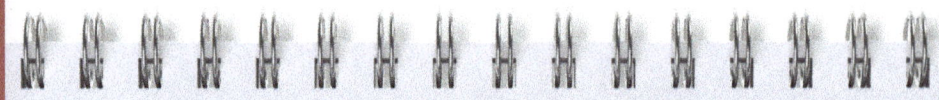

DRILL 1   TURN AND DIVE (BETWEEN THE LEGS) - LEVEL 1

Description The goalkeeper stands facing the assistant (2 meters apart).

The assistant throws the ball between the legs of the goalkeeper.

The goalkeeper turns swiftly and dives towards the ball.

The goalkeeper must turn from both sides. 10 repetitions.

Coaching Points

1. The goalkeeper turns swiftly.
2. Steady head.
3. Locate the ball quickly.
4. Both hands are going towards the ball.
5. One hand behind the ball, the other above it.
6. We grip the ball and secure it to our chest.

Turn swiftly, locate ball and go towards ball with both hands

Created using SoccerTutor.com Tactics Manager

Goalkeeper Training Methodology

DRILL 2 — FORWARD DIVE (BETWEEN THE LEGS) - LEVEL 1

Description The goalkeeper stands with his back facing towards the assistant (2 meters apart).

The assistant throws the ball between (or next to) his legs.

When the goalkeeper sees the ball, he must react and dive forward.

10 repetitions.

Coaching Points

1. Locate the ball quickly.
2. The goalkeeper must react quickly towards the ball with or without a step.
3. Extend hands towards the ball.
4. We grip the ball and secure it to our chest.
5. Be prepared to move your feet quickly if the ball passes by quickly.

See, locate, react and dive forward

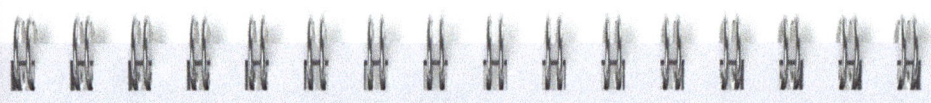

DRILL 3 — TURNING AFTER THOWING THE BALL UNDER THE LEGS (LEVEL 1)

Description The goalkeeper stands with his back turned to an assistant who is approximately 5 meters away and in a door opening (cone gate). The goalkeeper holds a ball in his hands and serves it with force under his legs towards the assistant. As soon as the goalkeeper serves the ball, he makes a fast 180-degree turn and reacts to the assistant's shot. Each goalkeeper must repeat the drill 10 times.

Coaching Points

1. The goalkeeper must turn quickly and quickly locate the ball.
2. Head should be kept steady and body weight should be placed forward.
3. Wait for the shot and do not drop to the ground too soon.
4. Be prepared if the speed of the ball is high.
5. Decide correctly whether to block or clear the ball.
6. Decide correctly which part of the body to clear the ball with.
7. If you block the ball it must be secured to the chest.
8. Be prepared to make a second save if necessary.

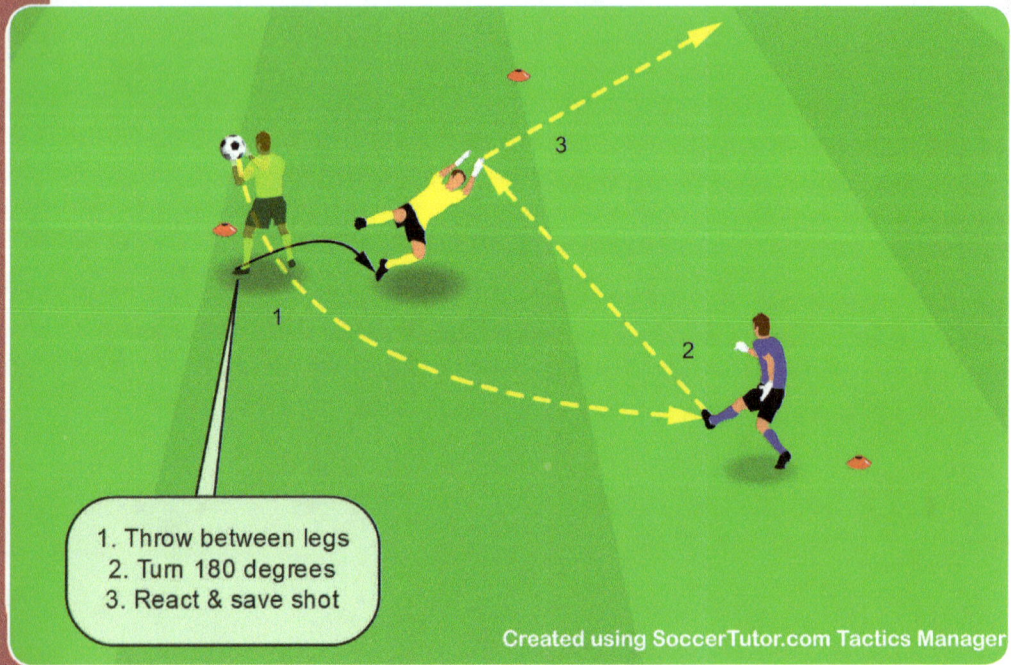

1. Throw between legs
2. Turn 180 degrees
3. React & save shot

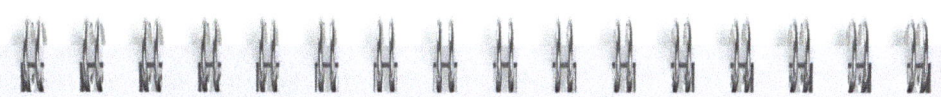

DRILL 4   TURN AND DROP (LEVEL 2)

Description The goalkeeper stands in the goal with his back turned away from the pitch. An assistant is outside the 6-yard box with balls.

The assistant will order the goalkeeper to turn around.

The goalkeeper must then quickly respond to balls that are served to him (with hands or feet) towards all directions in an attempt to score a goal.

Each goalkeeper will turn in both directions during the drill.

Each goalkeeper must repeat the drill 10 times.

Coaching Points
The same as the previous drill.

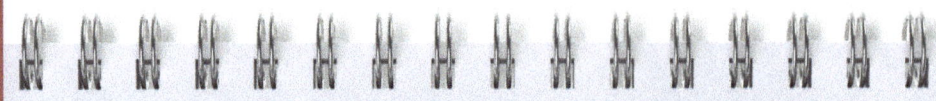

DRILL 5 — TURN BACK FROM POST TO SAVE SHOT (LEVEL 2)

Description The goalkeeper is at the post and facing sideways. One assistant stands at the side of the 6-yard box across with balls in his hands (close to the post). A second assistant stands in line with the center of the goal and to the side of the goalkeeper. The first assistant serves medium height balls to the second assistant who kicks the ball towards the goal as the goalkeeper turns. The goalkeeper moves parallel to the path of the ball and tries to make a save to parry the ball away.

Each goalkeeper must repeat the drill 10 times. Depending on the experience of the goalkeeper, the level of difficulty of the shots can increase.

Coaching Points
1. The goalkeeper must turn quickly and the head must be held steady.
2. He must quickly locate the ball and be in a good starting position after the turn.
3. Body weight should be forward and extend yourself to maximize your size.
4. Decide correctly whether to catch or parry the ball.
5. Decide correctly which part of the body to parry the ball with.
6. If you catch the ball it must be secured to the chest.
7. Be prepared to make a second save if necessary.

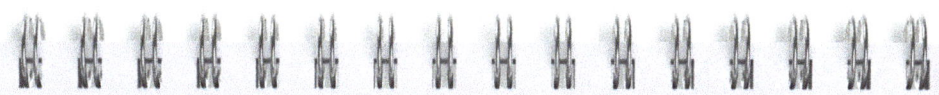

DRILL 6   TURN BACK FROM POST TO SAVE HEADER (LEVEL 2)

Description The goalkeeper is at the post and facing sideways. One assistant stands at the side of the 6-yard box across with balls in his hands (close to the post).

A second assistant stands in line with the center of the goal and to the side of the goalkeeper.

The first assistant serves high balls to the second assistant who heads the ball towards the goal as the goalkeeper turns. The goalkeeper moves parallel to the path of the ball and tries to clear it.

Each goalkeeper must repeat the drill 10 times.

Advice Depending on the experience of the goalkeeper, the level of difficulty of the shots can increase.

Coaching Points
The same as the previous drill.

REACTIONS

DRILL 7 — TURN BACK FROM POST TO SAVE HARD REBOUND SHOTS (LEVEL 3)

Description The goalkeeper is at the post and facing sideways. One assistant stands at the side of the 6-yard box with balls at his feet (close to the post). A second assistant is in the center around the penalty spot.

The first assistant serves a hard pass to the second assistant who in turn kicks the ball towards the goal. The goalkeeper moves parallel to the path of the ball and tries to catch or parry it. Each goalkeeper must repeat the drill 10 times.

Coaching Points
1. The goalkeeper must turn quickly and the head must be held steady.
2. He must quickly locate the ball and be in a good starting position after the turn.
3. Align yourself with the direction of the ball with body weight placed forward.
4. Extend yourself to maximize your size.
5. Select the correct technique, decide correctly whether to catch or parry the ball.
6. Decide correctly which part of the body to parry the ball with. If you block the ball it must be secured to the chest.
7. Be prepared to make a second save if necessary.

CHAPTER 11

DEALING WITH CROSSES

Breakaways (goalkeeper coming off his goal line) are no doubt the most difficult situation for the goalkeeper, and this is because it demands critical decisions in combination with the use of good technique under pressure. There are many stages of approach:

1. Initial position.
2. Communication with the defenders.
3. Reading the ball path and ball height.
4. Decision of going for the ball or staying.
5. Communication and decision making.
6. The technique we will use for the ball: catching, punching or change the path of the ball with the fingers

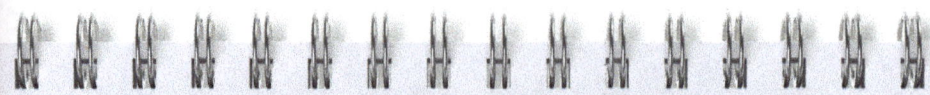

DRILL 1   HIGH BALL FORWARD (LEVEL 1)

Description The goalkeeper is by the post. The assistant stands with a ball in his hands around the penalty spot.

The assistant serves high forward balls to the goalkeeper and he in turn moves forward and performs front high catches.

Every goalkeeper does 10 repetitions.

Coaching Points

1. Watch the speed and the height of the ball as it moves.
2. Make small steps and run with hands out.
3. Jump with one foot and use the knee for protection.
4. Catch the ball at the highest point of its path.
5. Catching of the ball should always be done in your visual horizon.
6. Use the "W" handle to catch the ball and and clutch it to the chest.

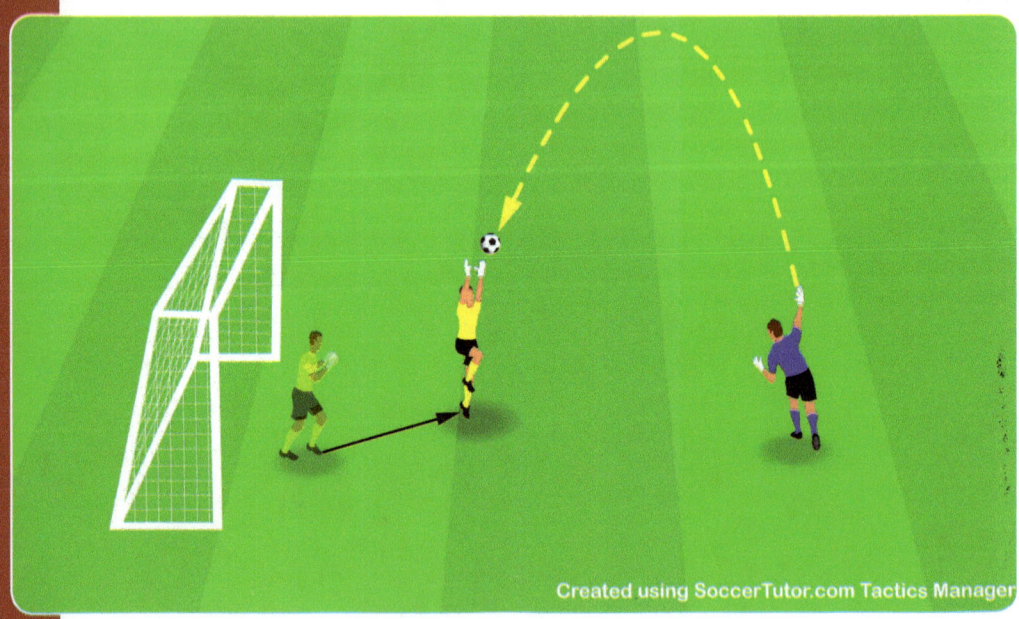

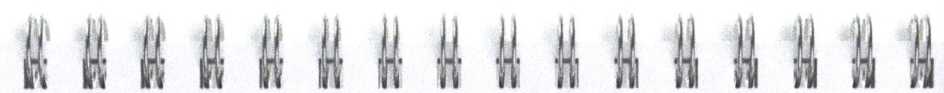

DRILL 2 HIGH BALL BACKWARDS (LEVEL 1)

Description The goalkeeper is positioned centrally on the edge of the 6-yard box. The assistant stands with a ball in hands around the penalty spot.

The assistant serves a high ball over and behind the goalkeeper and makes him moves backwards to catch the ball.

Advice 1 The steps that the goalkeeper makes are two at a time, defined by the assistant - cross-step left / cross-step right. Every goalkeeper does 10 repetitions.

Advice 2 The steps back are indicated for small shifts backwards and only when the goalkeeper is close to the goal. If you can't block the ball, you can parry it with the fingers over the post.

Coaching Points

The same as the previous drill.

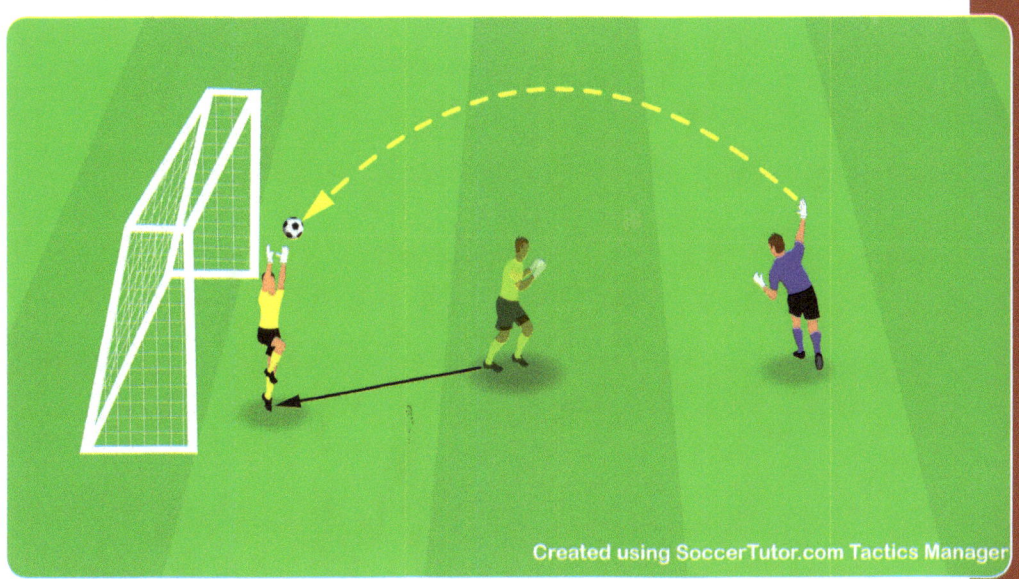

DEALING WITH CROSSES

3a drill

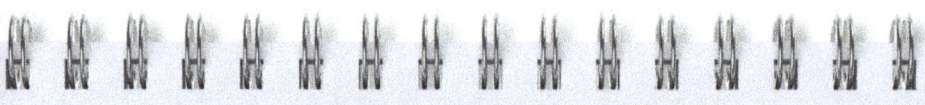

DRILL 3A   TOUCH OVER THE POST WHEN IN THE GOAL (LEVEL 1)

Description When the ball is close to the crossbar and it is difficult to block, the goalkeeper must tip the ball over the crossbar with his fingers.

Advice 1 The goalkeeper parries the ball away by using both hands in turn.

Advice 2 The flight of the ball should be high and far from the goal-post.

Coaching Points

1. Good initial position.
2. Take a good position so that you control all the possible paths of the ball. 3. Watch the speed and the height of the ball that moves.
4. Jump and parry the ball at the highest point of its flight.
5. Send the ball away with the fingers by parrying the ball over the crossbar at the greatest height possible.

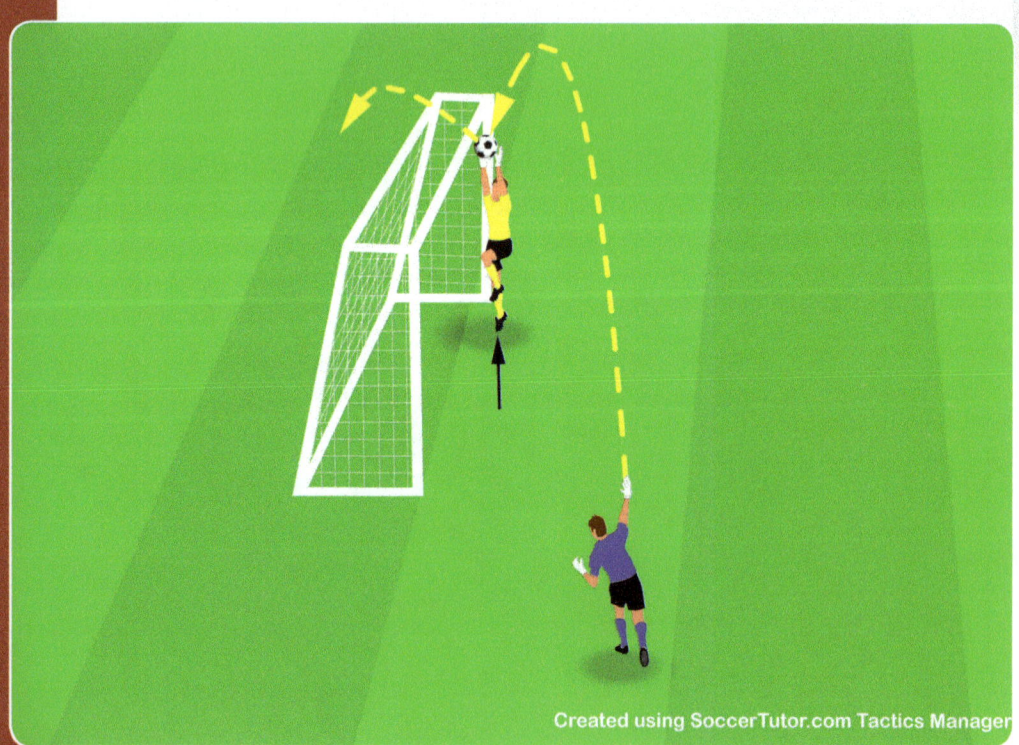

Goalkeeper Training Methodology

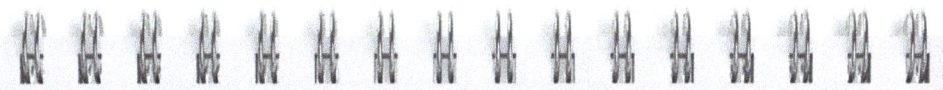

DRILL 3B   TOUCH OVER THE POST WHEN MOVING BACKWARDS (LEVEL 1)

When the ball is close to the crossbar and difficult to catch, the goalkeeper must tip the ball over the crossbar with his fingers.

Description The goalkeeper is in the center of the goal and assistant stands with ball in hands around the penalty spot. The assistant serves high balls over and behind the goalkeeper and makes him move backwards to tip the ball over the crossbar with his fingers.

Advice 1 The goalkeeper parries the ball away by using both hands in turn.

Advice 2 The flight of the ball should be high and far from the goal-post.

Coaching Points

1. Watch the speed and the height of the ball while it moves.
2. Jump and parry the ball at the highest point of its flight.
3. Send the ball away with the fingers by parrying the ball over the crossbar at the greatest height possible.

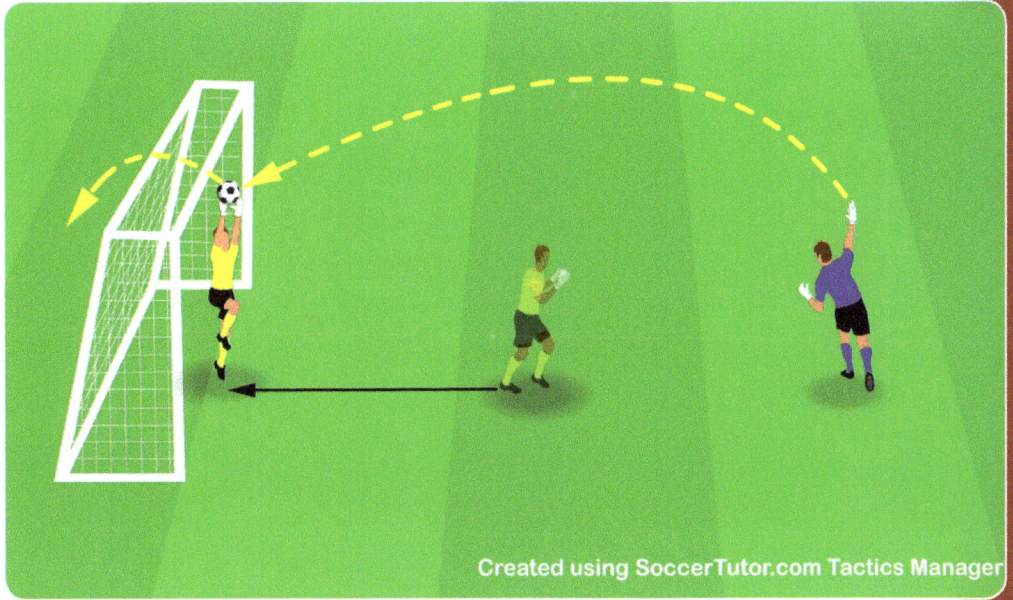

DEALING WITH CROSSES

DRILL 4   **DEALING WITH HIGH BALLS IN A STATIC POSITION AGAINST AN OPPONENT (LEVEL 1)**

This drill presents the obstruction that can happen to the goalkeeper from an opposition player when he goes to catch a high ball.

Description The assistant holds one ball in his hands and throws it high in the air. The goalkeeper who stands next to him does a spot leap to catch the ball. The assistant obstructs the goalkeeper with his body though physical contact.

Coaching Points

1. Watch the ball while it moves.
2. Jump with both feet.
3. Catch the ball at the highest point.
4. Use the "W" handle to catch the ball. Stretch your body towards the ball.

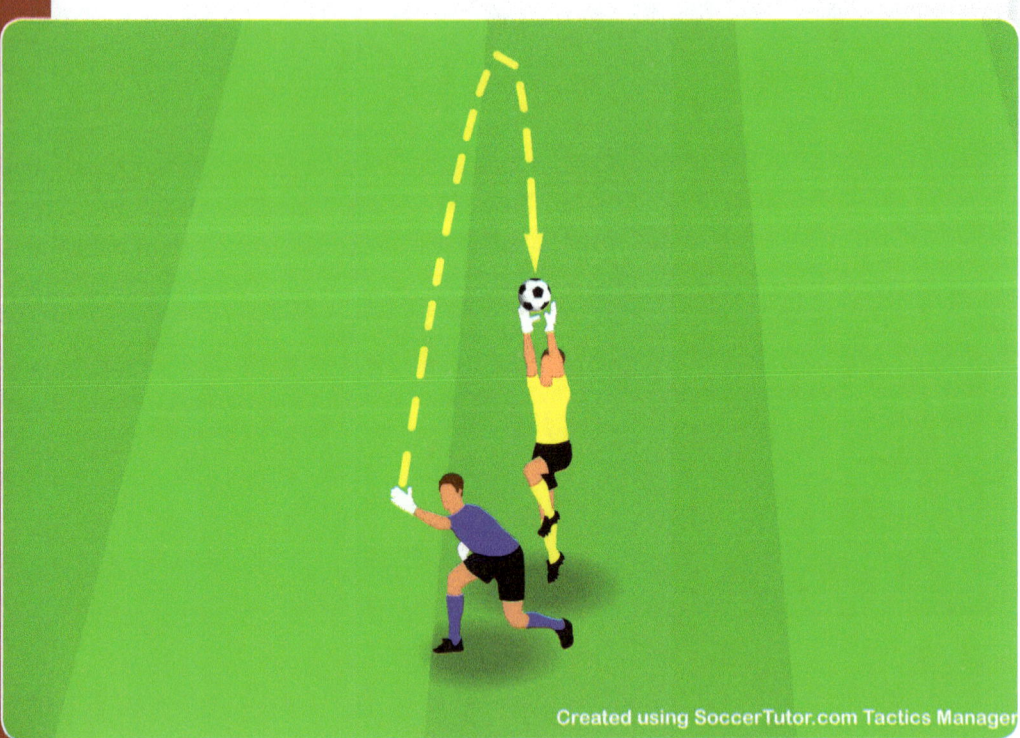

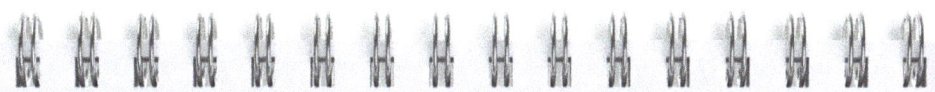

DRILL 5A   PUNCH FROM A FACE DOWN POSITION (LEVEL 1)

Striking the ball with a punch is a technique that every goalkeeper has to learn. The aim is to send the ball far and high.

Description The goalkeeper is face down on the ground as shown in the image below and looks at the assistant who is almost 2 meters away. The assistant serves the ball to the goalkeeper with his hands, so that the goalkeeper returns the ball with a single punch.

10 repetitions with each hand.

Coaching Points
1. Keep the wrist steady.
2. Hit the ball with the flat surface of the fist.
3. Hit the ball on the bottom half, so that it will take height after the hit.
4. We do not try to hit the ball with all our strength, but to hit it with the right technique and in the right direction.

5a drill

2

3

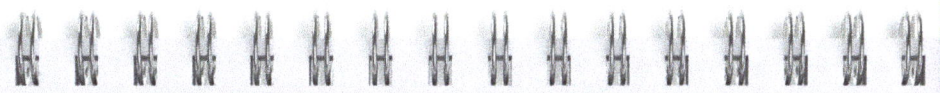

DRILL 5B   PUNCHES FROM A SITTING POSITION (LEVEL 1)

Description The goalkeeper sits on the ground and looks at the assistant who is 2 meters away.

The assistant serves the ball to the goalkeeper with his hands, so that the goalkeeper returns the ball with a single hand or double handed punch. The assistant throws the ball in varied areas but also with bounces on the ground. The goalkeeper must decide to hit the ball with one or two hands.

Coaching Points

1. Keep the wrist steady.
2. Hit the ball with the flat surface of the fist.
3. Hit the ball on the bottom half, so that it will take height after the hit.
4. We do not try to hit the ball with all our strength, but to hit it with the right technique and in the right direction.

drill 5b

2

3

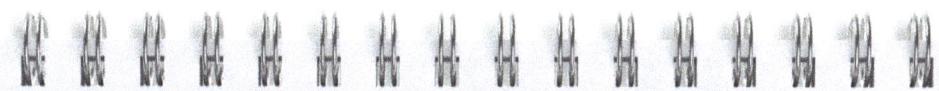

DRILL 6   SINGLE HANDED PUNCHES IN PAIRS (LEVEL 2)

This drill tests the ability of the goalkeeper to direct the ball to a specific target at the right height.

Description Two goalkeepers stand opposite each other 3 meters apart. They transfer the ball to one another with single punches.

Advice The aim is to punch the ball as many times as possible.

Coaching Points

1. Keep the wrist steady.
2. Hit the ball with the flat surface of the fist.
3. Hit the ball on the bottom half, so that it will take height after the hit.
4. We do not try to hit the ball with all our strength, but to hit it with the right technique and in the right direction.

DEALING WITH CROSSES

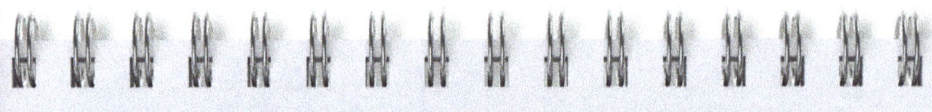

DRILL 7A   CROSSES CLOSE TO THE FRONT POST (LEVEL 2)

It is very important that the goalkeeper know the behavior of the ball, when it has different swerves (internal and external).

The knowledge of the appropriate techniques to deal with these situations must be educationally analyzed.

Description The goalkeeper is in the center of the goal and the assistant crosses the ball to the front post area.

The goalkeeper catches or punches the ball away.

Advice The position of the ball defines the goalkeeper's position at the post, e.g. toward the bottom corner or the center.

He never stands on the goal-line but outside of it - how far outside depends on the position of the ball.

The goalkeeper goes always to the ball.

Coaching Points The same as the next drill.

Cross to the front post

DRILL 7B CROSSES INSIDE THE 6-YARD BOX (LEVEL 2)

Description The goalkeeper is in the center of the goal and the assistant crosses the ball inside the 6-yard box. The goalkeeper catches or punches the ball away.

Advice The same as the previous drill.

Coaching Points

1. Good initial position, you take sideways steps to set up next position, so that you control all the possible paths of the ball.
2. Watch the speed and the height of the ball that moves.
3. Start with the external foot. Perform small and quick steps.
4. Jump and catch the ball at the highest point of its flight.
5. Bring the ball to the chest.
6. Shout at the breakaway.
7. The goalkeeper reacts when the ball leaves the player's foot.
8. Use the "W" handle to catch the ball or to punch it away with one or two hands.

Cross anywhere inside the 6-yard box

DEALING WITH CROSSES

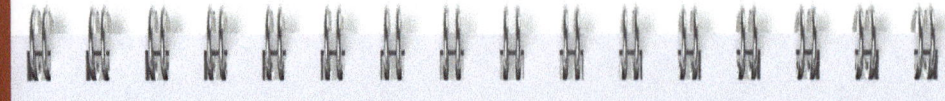

DRILL 7C — CROSSES OUTSIDE THE 6-YARD BOX (LEVEL 2)

Description The goalkeeper is in the center of the goal and the assistant crosses the ball towards the edge of the 6-yard box (outside).

The goalkeeper catches or punches the ball away.

Advice The same as the previous drill.

Coaching Points
The same as the previous drill.

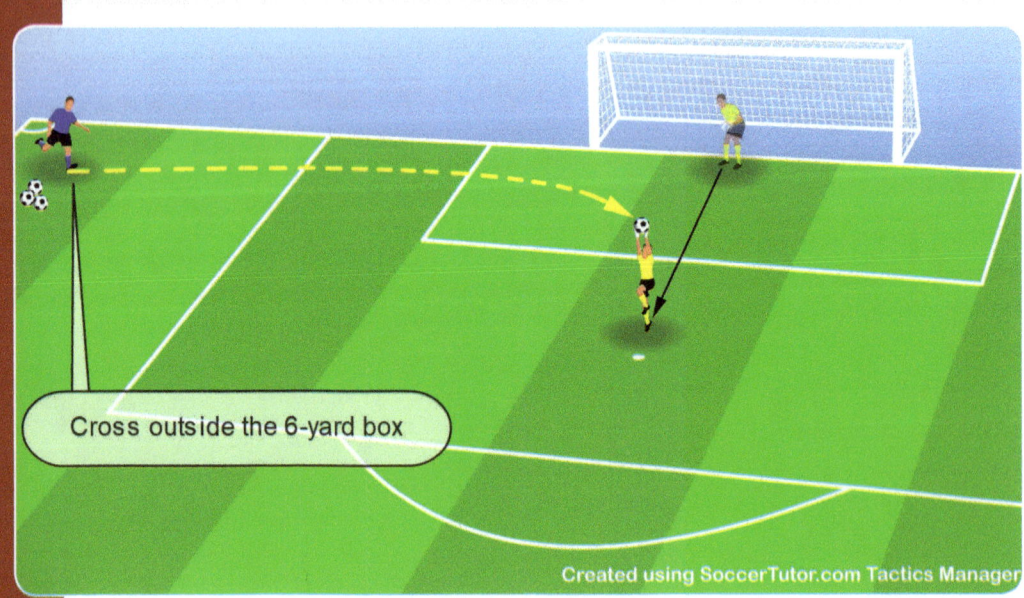

Cross outside the 6-yard box

DRILL 8   **DEALING WITH DIFFERENT CROSSES (LEVEL 2)**

The most crucial mistake that goalkeepers usually make when moving off their line to deal with a cross, is to react before the ball leaves the feet of the crosser. This usually causes a bad estimation of the ball's path/flight.

Description The goalkeeper is at the center of the goal and is directed to the balls that are in different spots.

The assistant makes crosses to different spots (front post, inside 6-yard box, outside 6-yard box).

The goalkeeper must estimate every ball separately and work accordingly.

Advice The same as the previous drill.

Coaching Points
The same as the previous drill.

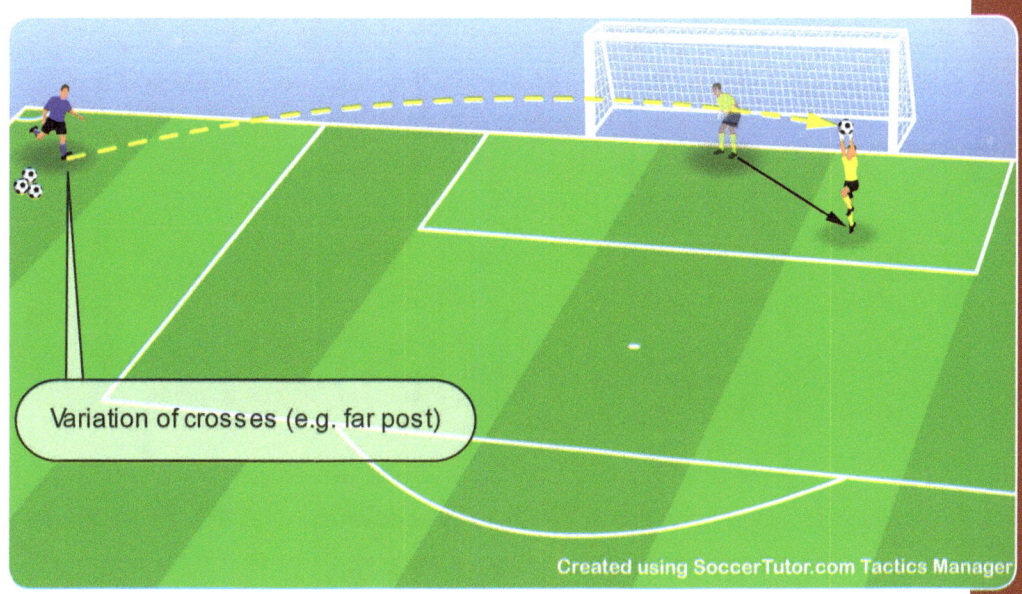

Variation of crosses (e.g. far post)

DRILL 9   CROSSES WITH THE HELP OF A DEFENDER (LEVEL 2)

After we have made trained for different kinds of crosses, it is very useful to continue the training by creating more realistic situations. It is a very good idea to use a defender with whom the goalkeeper must cooperate and choose which balls he will take and which the defender will take.

Description The goalkeeper is in the center of the goal and the assistant delivers crosses into different areas. In front of the goalkeeper is a defender. The goalkeeper must assess every ball separately and work accordingly in cooperation with the defender.

Advice The goalkeeper must decide which balls are his and which he will leave to the defender. If he decides to come out of his goal, he must shout loud and clear, so that he will warn the defender of his action. Communication is key.

Coaching Points

1. Good initial position, you take sideways steps to set up next position, so that you control all the possible paths of the ball.
2. Guide the defender to take the most appropriate position.
3. Watch the speed and the height of the ball.
4. Start with the external foot. Perform small and quick steps.
5. Jump, catch or parry away the ball at the highest point of its flight.
7. The goalkeeper reacts as soon as the ball leaves the player's foot.
8. Use the "W" handling to catch the ball.
9. Shout your decisions - if you want to deal with the cross shout "KEEPER'S" and when you want the defender to clear the ball shout "AWAY".

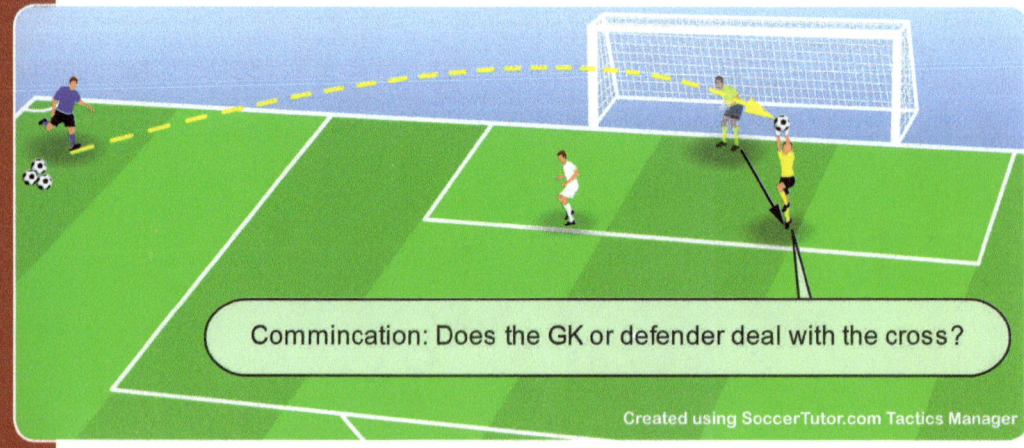

Commincation: Does the GK or defender deal with the cross?

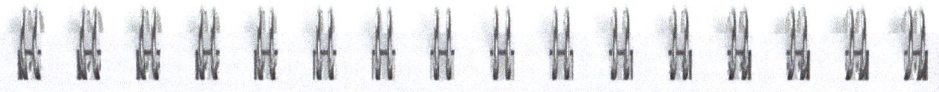

DRILL 10A   DEALING WITH CROSSES AGAINST AN OPPONENT (LEVEL 1)

The presence of the attacker increases the pressure on the goalkeeper.

Description The goalkeeper is in the center of the goal. In front of him there is an assistant who stands still and plays the role of the attacker. The second assistant serves the balls high and close to the attacker who stands still. This forces the goalkeeper to come out of goal and make physical contact with the attacker. The goalkeeper chooses whether to catch or punch the ball away.

Advice The goalkeeper always goes to the ball.

Coaching Points

1. Good initial position, you take sideways steps to set up next position, so that you control all the possible paths of the ball.
2. Watch the speed and height of the ball.
3. Start with the external foot. Perform small and quick steps.
4. Jump and catch the ball at the highest point.
5. Bring the ball into the chest.
6. Shout "KEEPER'S" when initially moving forward.

Catch ball against stationary opponent

DEALING WITH CROSSES

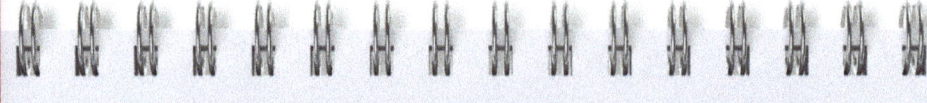

DRILL 10B DEALING WITH CROSSES AGAINST AN OPPONENT (LEVEL 2)

Description The goalkeeper is in the center of the goal. In front of him there is an assistant who stands still and plays the role of the attacker.

The other assistant delivers crosses from the corner.

The goalkeeper chooses to catch or punch the ball away. The attacker tries to score.

Advice 1 The goalkeeper shouldn't be distracted by the attacker's moves. His eyes must be fixed on the ball.

Advice 2 There are situations when the goalkeeper is unable to catch or punch the ball. He must then stretch his body toward the path of the ball and change the path with his fingers.

Coaching Points

The same as the previous drill.

Catch or punch the ball against an opponent trying to score

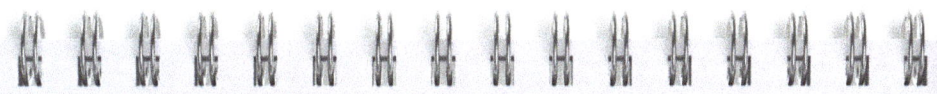

DRILL 11 — CROSSES WITH THE HELP OF A DEFENDER AGAINST AN OPPONENT (LEVEL 3)

Description The goalkeeper is in the center of the goal. In front of him there is a defender and an attacker. The assistant crosses the ball and the goalkeeper is asked to react - whether to come out of goal and deal with the cross or leave the ball for the defender to deal with.

Advice (1) The goalkeeper shouldn't be distracted by the attacker's moves. His eyes must be fixed on the ball. (2) When the goalkeeper decides to come out of goal, the defender must obstruct the attacker from getting close to the goalkeeper. (3) Communication between the goalkeeper and defender is key.

Coaching Points

1. Good initial position, you take sideways steps to set up next position, so that you control all the possible paths of the ball.
2. Watch the speed and height of the ball.
3. Start with the external foot. Perform small and quick steps.
4. Jump and catch the ball at the highest point. Bring the ball into the chest.
5. Shout your decisions - if you want to deal with the cross shout "KEEPER'S" and when you want the defender to clear the ball shout "AWAY".
6. The goalkeeper reacts as soon as the ball leaves the player's foot.

Defend cross with help from defender (leave, catch, punch etc)

DEALING WITH CROSSES

CHAPTER 12

DISTRIBUTION

Since the goalkeeper has the ball he is like all the other players. It is very important to use the ball correctly. The goalkeeper must know all the different distribution techniques: close or far, with the hands or feet.

It is very important that the goalkeeper understands where, when, why and which technique he must use.

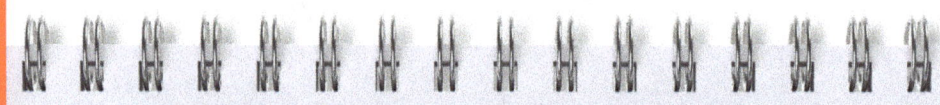

DRILL 1   ROLL OUT ON THE GROUND (LEVEL 1)

Rolling out on the ground is used for close distances. The technique is very simple and has as a basic rule that the ball touches the ground the whole way.

Description The goalkeeper practices rolling balls to an assistant who is 10 meters away near the sideline.

The technique is very simple and has as a basic rule for the ball to touch the ground for the whole duration of its travel. To achieve this the goalkeeper must bend his knee.

When the goalkeeper is familiar with the delivery to a static target, we ask the assistant to make a move from one cone to another (image 2). The purpose is for the goalkeeper to pass the ball to the feet of the assistant while he is running.

Coaching Points

1. The front foot must show the direction we want to roll the ball to.
2. Use a bowling technique. Stay low when you throw the ball. Ensure the smooth path of the ball.
3. Do not increase the difficulty rate for your teammates to receive the ball, so deliver the ball at the right speed.

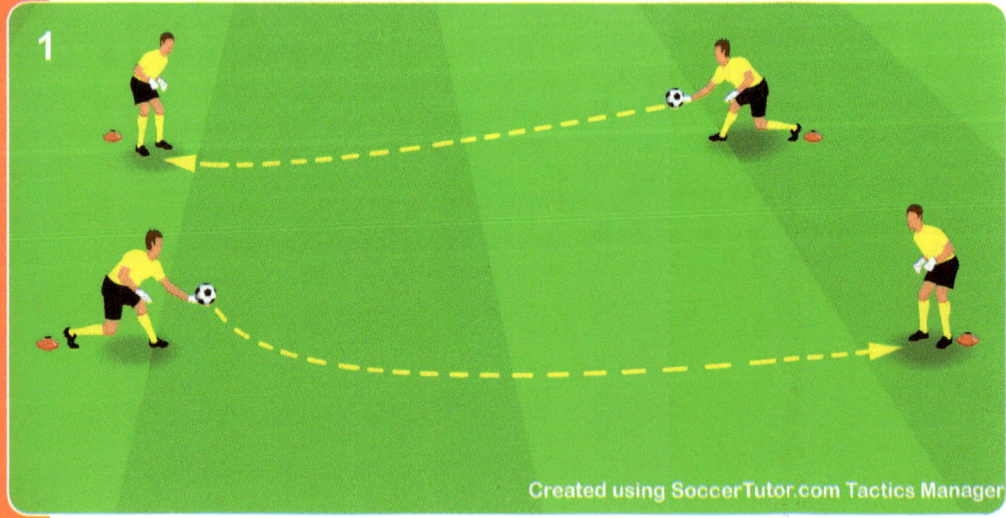

DISTRIBUTION

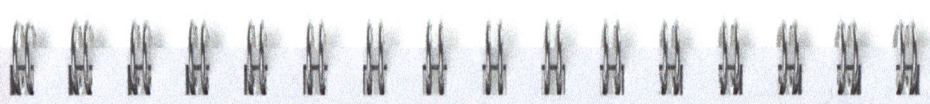

DRILL 2   THROW OUT WITH BOUNCE (LEVEL 1)

Throwing out over the shoulder with a bounce is for middle distances. The path of the ball is straight.

Description The goalkeeper throws the balls over the shoulder and it bounces once on the way to an assistant who 10 meters away.

When the goalkeeper is familiar with the delivery to a static target, we ask the assistant to make a move from one cone to another.

The purpose is for the goalkeeper to pass the ball to the feet of the assistant while he is running.

Coaching Points

1. The front foot must show the direction we want to throw the ball to.
2. Stay low when you throw the ball.
3. The bouncing of the ball should be roughly at 2-3 meters from the player.
4. The ball must be delivered without spin, so that it will not increase the difficulty rate for the player to receive.

DRILL 3A THROW OVER THE SHOULDER (LEVEL 1)

Throwing out over the shoulder (without a bounce) is for large distances. It is useful because the goalkeeper can throw the ball with great accuracy to areas where he can't deliver it with low balls.

Description The goalkeeper throws the ball high and straight over the shoulder to an assistant who is approximately 10 meters away.

When the goalkeeper is familiar with the delivery to a static target, we ask the assistant to make a move from one cone to another.

The purpose is for the goalkeeper to pass the ball to the feet of the assistant while he is running.

Coaching Points

1. The front foot and hand must be directed to where we want to throw the ball to.
2. The back hand, with the ball, makes a ballistic move along the arm.
3. We speed up with bigger force on the ball to carry the longer distance.

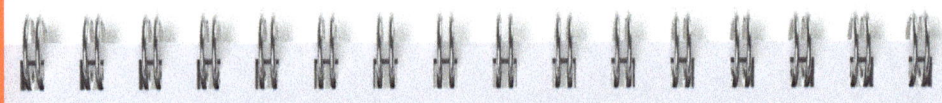

DRILL 3B   LONG THROW OVER AN OPPONENT (LEVEL 1)

Description The goalkeeper throws the ball over the shoulder to an assistant who is approximately 20 -30 meters away. In between, there is a second assistant who plays the role of the opponent.

The goalkeeper throws the ball over the opponent who is between them.

Advice 1 Make sure to do a comprehensive warm up of the shoulders.

Advice 2 The ball should not be thrown too high.

Coaching Points
1. The front foot must point to the direction we want to throw the ball.
2. The back hand, with the ball, makes a ballistic move along the arm.
3. We speed up with bigger force on the ball to carry the longer distance.
4. Throw to the front foot of your teammate.

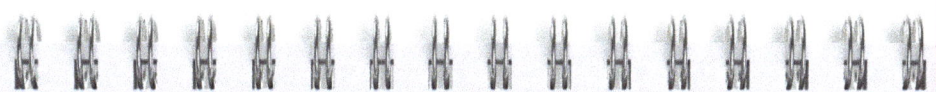

DRILL 4 CATCH A CROSS AND SWITCH PLAY (LEVEL 2)

Description The goalkeeper reacts to a cross from the side.

After catching the ball, he turns to the opposite side and throws the ball to a teammate who moves forward to receive.

The kind of throw needed will depend on the distance of the teammate.

Advice It is very important that the goalkeeper throws the ball to the front foot or just in front of his teammate.

Only with this way he will not delay the development of the game and we will not force the teammate to stop or move backwards.

Coaching Point
The front foot must point to the direction we want to throw the ball.

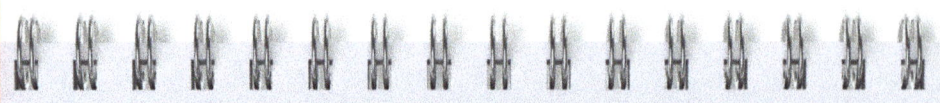

DRILL 5 — PASSING FROM A STATIONARY POSITION ALONG THE GROUND (LEVEL 1)

Description The goalkeeper passes the ball with his feet at a 15-20 meter distance.

The goalkeeper's passes must have the right accuracy toward the target.

Advice 1 We work with both feet.

Advice 2 The torso remains steady. The shoulders point towards the ball path.

Coaching Points

1. The approach to the ball is in at an angle.
2. Place the back foot sideways and behind the ball.
3. The part of the foot that hits the ball points outward and ankle remains stretched.

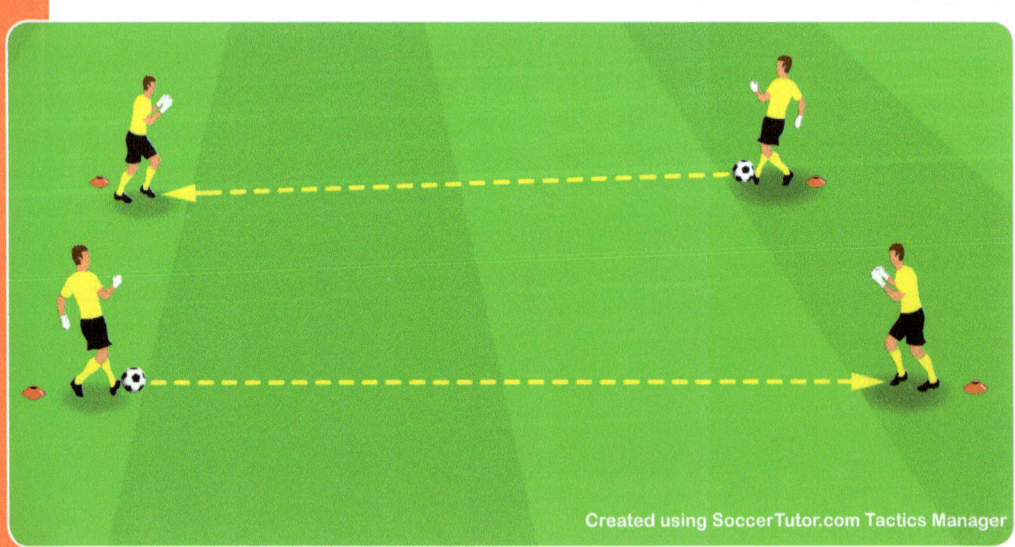

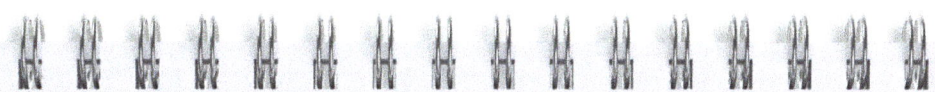

DRILL 6 — LONG PASSING WITH RUN UP (LEVEL 1)

This pass is usually used when the goalkeeper:

1) Wants to keep the high pace.

2) His team is under pressure.

3) When he wants to clear the ball out of the box and gain meters up the pitch.

Description The goalkeeper leaves the ball on the ground and while moving he kicks the ball 15-20 meters. The goalkeeper's kicks must have the right height and accuracy toward the target.

Advice The goalkeeper leaves it on the ground, always in front and side-on from the foot that will kick the ball. We work with both feet.

Coaching Points

1. The same as the previous drill.
2. The eyes see the ball and the head is steady.
3. Loose movement and move at pace to the ball.

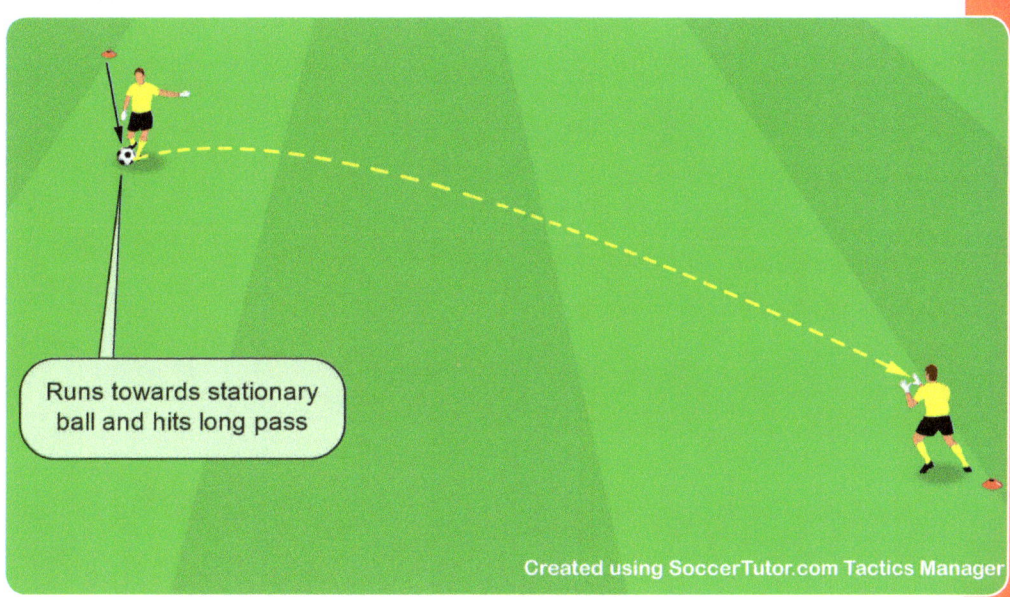

Runs towards stationary ball and hits long pass

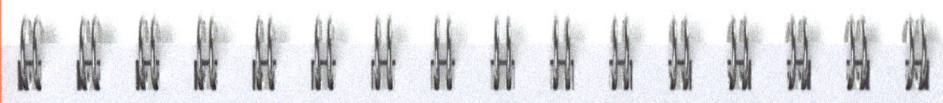

DRILL 7 — SIDE-ON VOLLEY KICK OUT (LEVEL 1)

The volley is the most common form of distribution from the goalkeeper, for hitting targets in the other half of the pitch.

With the right technique, the ball can travel long distances without big height.

Description The goalkeeper practices the volley technique with a 30-40 meter target. The kicks of the goalkeeper must have the right height and accuracy toward the target.

Advice The goalkeeper drops the ball onto the foot with the opposite hand and then kicks through the ball sideways. We work with both feet. You can work on all the volley techniques.

Coaching Points

1. The same as the previous drill.
2. The eyes see the ball and the head is steady.

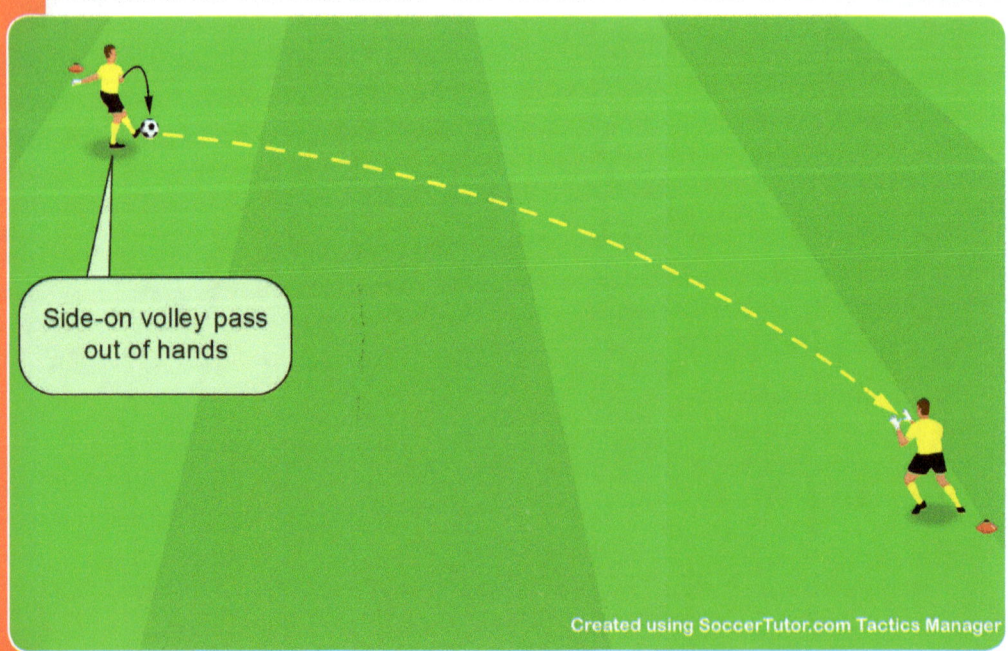

Side-on volley pass out of hands

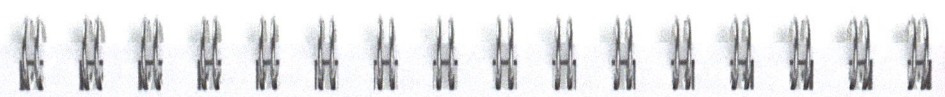

DRILL 8   CATCH AND DISTRIBUTE (LEVEL 2)

Description Two goalkeepers are approximately 25 meters apart and within two 5 x 5 meter squares. In the middle there is an assistant with a ball. The assistant kicks the ball into the hands of one of the two goalkeepers. The goalkeeper catches the ball. He then leaves it on the ground and kicks the ball to the other goalkeeper. The second goalkeeper receives the ball and passes it to the assistant (or rolls it).

Advice 1 The ball travels over the assistant and is aimed at the other goalkeeper to receive within the square.

Advice 2 The goalkeeper positions the ball sideways from the foot that will execute the kick. We work with both feet.

Coaching Points

1. Place the back foot sideways and behind the ball.
2. The part of the foot that hits the ball points outward and ankle remains stretched.
3. The eyes see the ball and the head is steady.
4. Loose movement and move at pace to the ball.

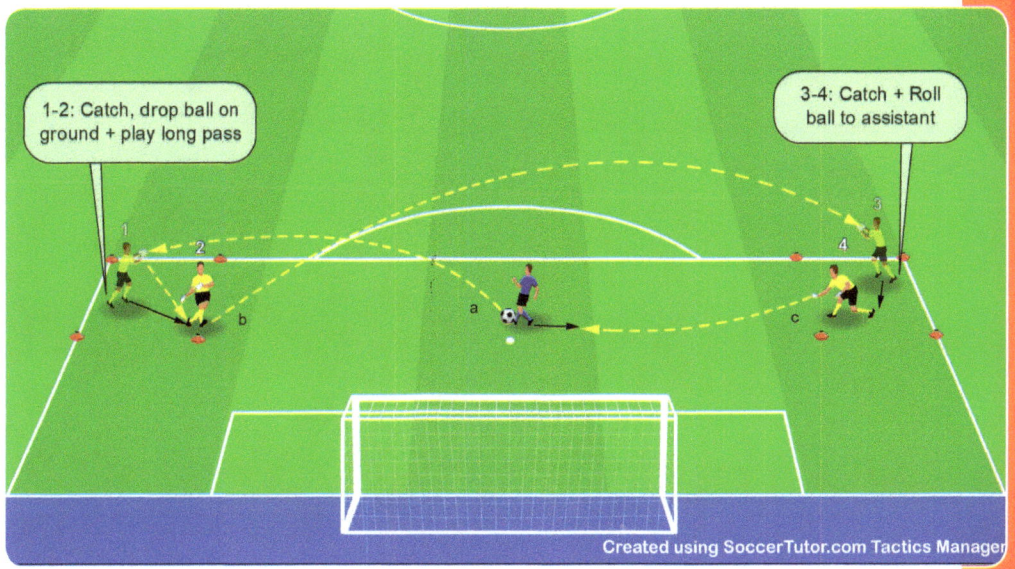

DISTRIBUTION

DRILL 9 CATCH AND DISTRIBUTE WITH SIDE-ON VOLLEY (LEVEL 2)

Description Two goalkeepers are approximately 25 meters apart and within two 5 x 5 meter squares.

In the middle, there is an assistant with a ball. The assistant kicks the ball into the hands of one of the two goalkeepers.

The goalkeeper catches the ball. He then kicks it out of his hands (side-on kick) to the other goalkeeper. The second goalkeeper receives the ball and passes it to the assistant (or rolls it).

Advice 1 Make the right handling techniques to catch long balls.

Advice 2 The goalkeeper places the ball sideways from the foot that will execute the kick. We work with both feet. Work on all the volley techniques.

Coaching Points
The same as the previous drill.

CHAPTER 13

BACK PASSES

For back passes, a very good first touch (receiving is required by the goalkeeper, in addition to good distribution of the ball, near or far. The goalkeeper must also use both feet.

The drills in this chapter work with the goalkeeper's feet. The warm-up and the recovery are the appropriate time for these drills. There are two phases for the back pass:

1) The preparation phase for the goalkeeper to receive the ball.
2) Distribution.

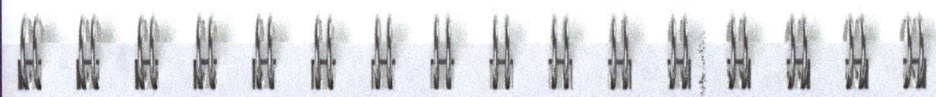

1a drill

DRILL 1A   THE SQUARE: RECEIVE AND PASS ON GROUND (LEVEL 1)

Description The goalkeeper is in a 2 x 2 meter square. The assistant is a few meters away with a ball at his feet.

The assistant passes rolling balls to the goalkeeper. The goalkeeper takes a touch to the side and out of the square, and then he passes the ball back to the assistant. The goalkeeper works with both feet (both sides).

Advice Move on tips of toes (like dancing). Move with small steps.

Coaching Points
1. Get in the line of the ball.
2. Keep your torso steady.
3. Control the ball with the outside of the foot.
4. Work on all the techniques to receive and pass.
5. Receiving should be done in the direction we want to move.
6. The center of gravity should follow the ball's path.
7. Precision on the return pass to the assistant.

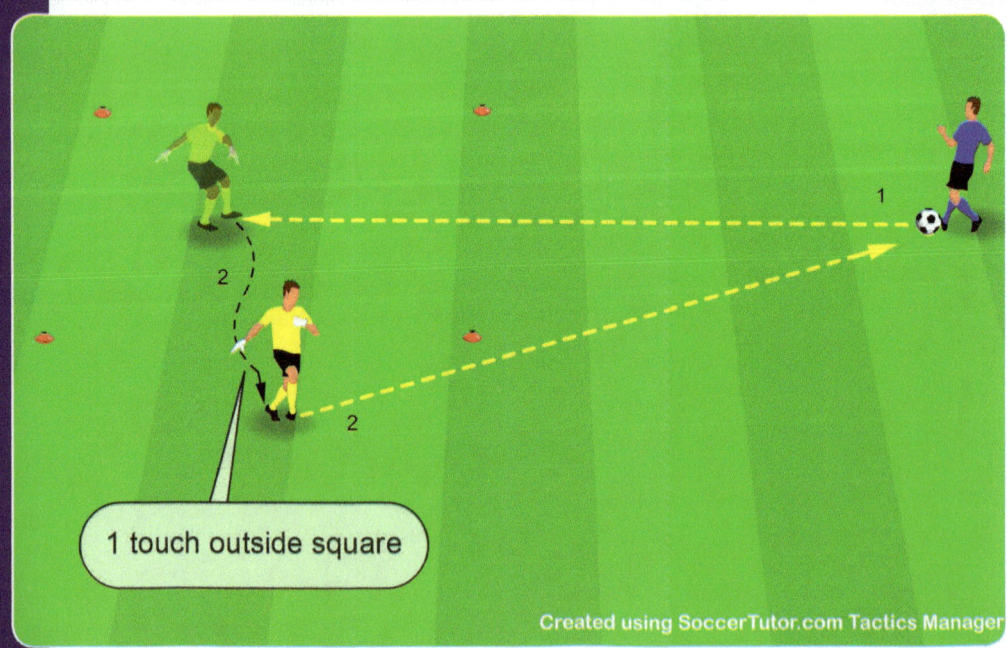

1 touch outside square

Created using SoccerTutor.com Tactics Manager

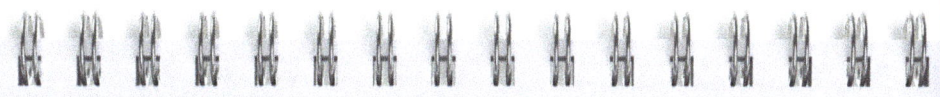

DRILL 1B   THE SQUARE: MEDIUM RANGE PASSES ON THE VOLLEY (LEVEL 1)

Description The goalkeeper is in a 2 x 2 meter square. The assistant is a few meters away with a ball in his hands.

The assistant serves medium range balls to the goalkeeper. The goalkeeper returns the balls to the assistant on the volley with medium kicks.

Work on all the kicking techniques. The goalkeeper works on both feet.

Advice Move on tips of toes (like dancing). Move with small steps.

Coaching Points

1. Get in the line of the ball.
2. Keep your torso steady.
3. Calculate the ball path.
4. Return the ball correctly to the assistant.

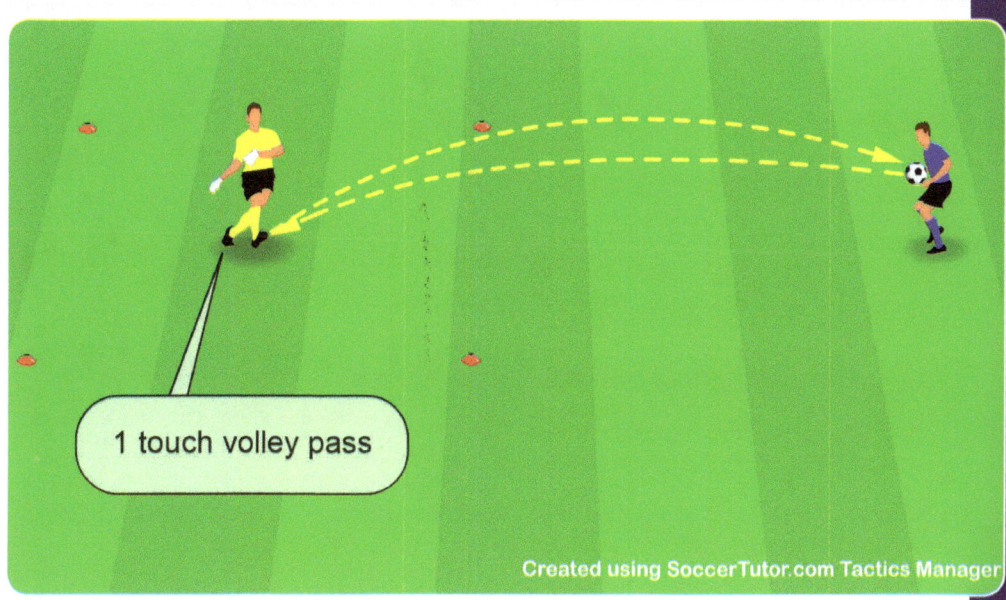

1 touch volley pass

1c drill

DRILL 1C   THE SQUARE: MEDIUM RANGE PASSES WITH BOUNCE (LEVEL 1)

Description The goalkeeper is in a 2 x 2 meter square. The assistant is a few meters away with a ball in his hands.

The assistant serves medium range balls to the goalkeeper. The goalkeeper must return the ball just after the ball makes a small bounce on the ground.

Work on all the kicking techniques. The goalkeeper works with both feet.

Advice Move on tips of toes (like dancing). Move with small steps.

Coaching Points

1. Get in the line of the ball.
2. Keep your torso steady.
3. Calculate the ball's path.
4. Connect with the ball from below so that it will take height.
5. Return the ball to the assistant's hands.

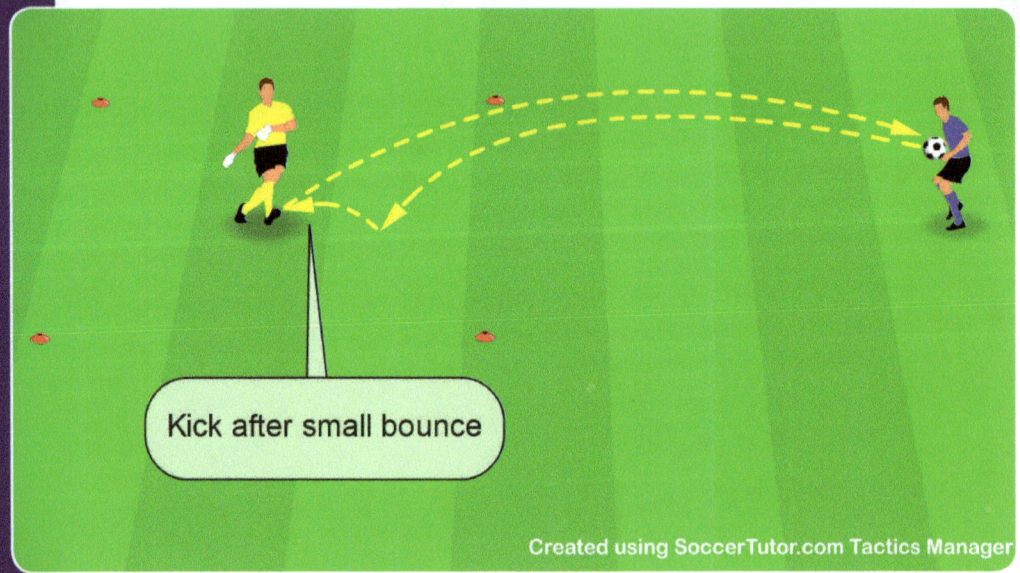

Kick after small bounce

Created using SoccerTutor.com Tactics Manager

Goalkeeper Training Methodology

DRILL 1D — THE SQUARE: PASSING AFTER 1, 2 OR 3 TOUCHES (LEVEL 1)

Description The goalkeeper is in a 2 x 2 meter square. The assistant is a few meters away with a ball in his hands. The assistant serves the ball freely to the goalkeeper. The goalkeeper returns the ball after taking one, two or three touches without leaving the square.

Advice Use all parts of your body for the pass back and for the first touch.

Coaching Points

1. Get in the line of the ball.
2. Keep your torso steady.
3. Choose which is the best passing choice and how many touches you will make.
4. Ensure precision of return pass (with all the body parts).
5. When you take the first touch, absorb the ball's force and place it sideways from your body.
6. Ensure good passing quality after the first touch.

GK can use 1, 2 or 3 touches and all parts of body to pass back

BACK PASSES

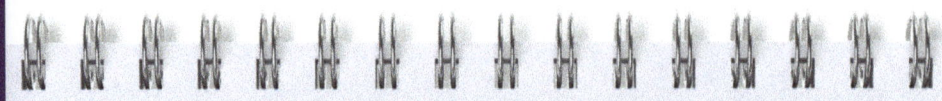

DRILL 2 — BACK PASS WITH PRESSURE (LEVEL 2)

Description The goalkeeper is in a 5 x 8 meter area in the penalty area. There are two assistants outside the area with balls.

One assistant passes a rolling ball to the goalkeeper and then follows the path of the ball to the goalkeeper, playing the role of the attacker who is after the ball.

The goalkeeper must act quickly by taking a first touch to the opposite side and then passing to the second assistant who is on the other side of the pitch.

Advice (1) Right body angle. (2) Check space. (3) Move on tips of toes and move with small steps. (4) Calculate the ball speed and the attacker's speed. (5) All the techniques of receiving and passing should be used.

Coaching Points

1. Get in the line of the ball.
2. Keep your torso steady.
3. The teammate must form a good passing angle.
4. Calculate your pass. Do not take a risk.

DRILL 3 — SWITCH PLAY (LEVEL 1)

Description The goalkeeper is on the edge of the 6-yard box. There are two assistants at an angle with a ball. One assistant rolls a ball to the goalkeeper. The goalkeeper receives the ball and passes it to the second assistant who is on the opposite side. The drill continues from the side the goalkeeper passed to.

Advice (1) Right body angle. (2) Check space. (3) Move on tips of toes and move with small steps. (4) Calculate the ball speed. (5) All the techniques of receiving and passing should be used.

Coaching Points
1. Get in the line of the ball.
2. Keep your torso steady.
3. Right body position (open).
4. The goalkeeper points with the hand on which foot he wants the ball.
5. Checking of the shoulder.
6. Good first touch.
7. Good distribution to the teammate, on the correct foot.
8. Support your teammate after the pass.

BACK PASSES

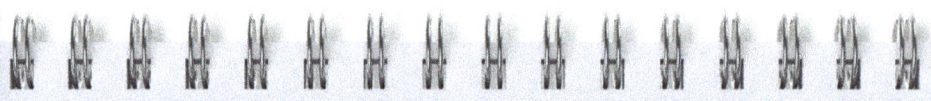

DRILL 4 — SWITCH PLAY WITH PRESSURE (LEVEL 2)

Description The goalkeeper is on the edge of the 6-yard box. There are two assistants at an angle with a ball.

One assistant rolls a ball to the goalkeeper. The goalkeeper receives the ball and passes it to the second assistant who is on the opposite side.

The drill continues from the side the goalkeeper passed to. Outside the penalty area, there is a third assistant who plays the role of the attacker. His aim is to press the goalkeeper for all the back passes.

Advice (1) Right body angle. (2) Check space. (3) Move on tips of toes and move with small steps. (4) Calculate the ball speed and the attacker's speed. (5) All the techniques of receiving and passing should be used. (6) Keep calm.

Coaching Points
The same as the previous drill.

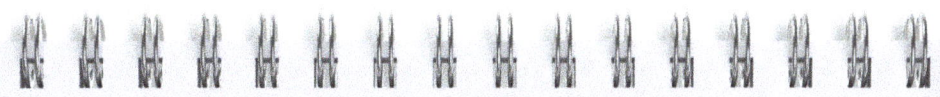

DRILL 5   DEALING WITH THE BACK PASS (LEVEL 2)

Description Two goalkeepers are approximately 25 meters apart and within two 5 x 5 meter squares. In the middle there is an assistant with a ball. The assistant passes the ball to one of the two goalkeepers. The first goalkeeper controls it and then passes the ball (over the assistant) to the second goalkeeper. The second goalkeeper receives the ball and with 2 or 3 touches passes the ball along the ground back to the central assistant. The assistant in turn returns the ball to the goalkeeper with one touch and he receives it and passes it to the other goalkeeper.

Advice (1) Move on tips of toes and with small steps. (2) Calculate the ball speed. (3) The goalkeeper's first touch is towards the foot that will execute the pass. (4) We work on both feet. (5) The ball needs to have good height to go over the assistant's head. (6) Keep calm.

Coaching Points
1. Get in the line of the ball.
2. Keep your torso steady.
3. Choose the best option for how many touches to take.
4. Good first touch.

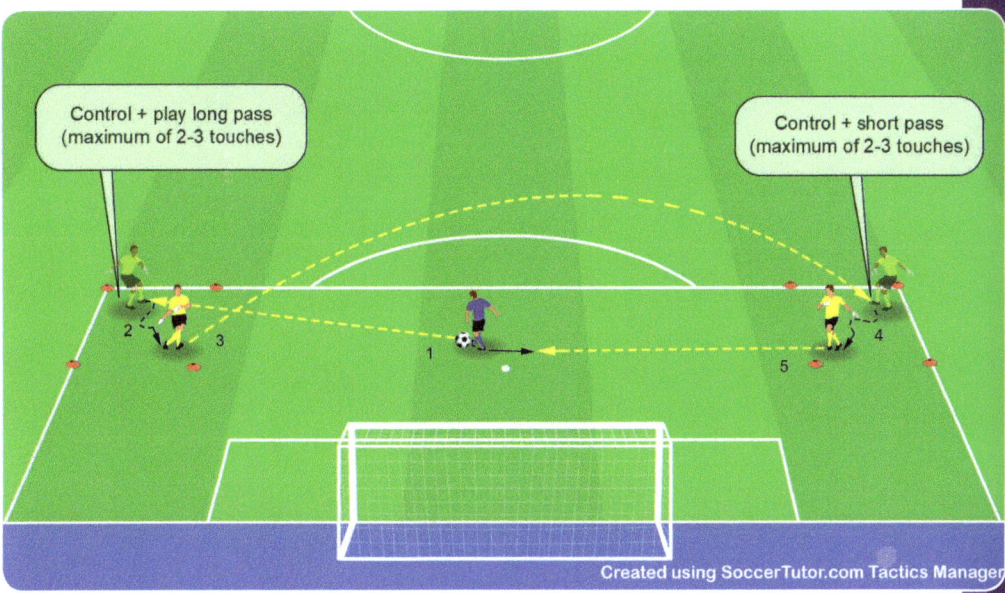

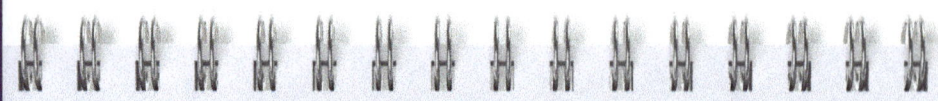

DRILL 6   **DEALING WITH BACK PASSES WITH 1 TOUCH (LEVEL 2)**

Description Two goalkeepers are approximately 25 meters apart and within two 5 x 5 meter squares. In the middle, there is an assistant with a ball. The assistant passes the ball to one of the two goalkeepers.

The first goalkeeper controls it and then passes the ball (over the assistant) to the second goalkeeper. The second goalkeeper receives the ball and with 1 or 2 touches passes the ball along the ground back to the central assistant.

The assistant then returns the ball to the goalkeeper with one touch and he receives it and passes it to the other goalkeeper.

Advice (1) Move on tips of toes and with small steps. (2) Calculate the ball speed. (3) Keep calm. (4) Work on both feet.

Coaching Points

1. Get in the line of the ball.
2. Keep your torso steady.
3. Good distribution to the other goalkeeper within the square.

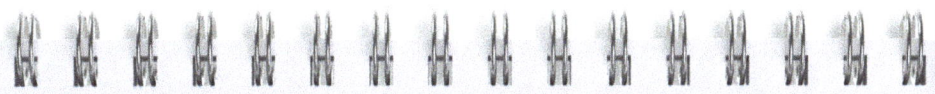

DRILL 7   DEALING WITH BACK PASSES UNDER PRESSURE (LEVEL 2)

Description This is exactly the same as the previous drill 6 but now we add a second assistant who applies pressure to the goalkeepers every time they receive a pass within a square.

Advice (1) Move on tips of toes and with small steps. (2) Calculate the ball speed. (3) Keep calm. (4) Work on both feet.

Coaching Points

The same as the previous drill.

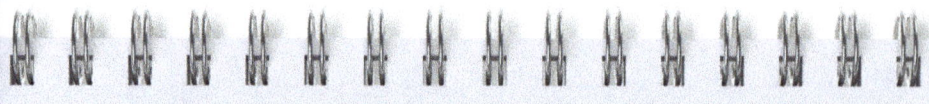

DRILL 8 — DECISION MAKING WHETHER TO DISTRIBUTE THE BALL SHORT OR LONG (LEVEL 3)

Description Two goalkeepers are approximately 25 meters apart and within two 5 x 5 meter squares. Between the goalkeepers there is a 16 x 8 meter area and there are two assistants - one plays as a teammate and the other plays as an opponent. The drill begins with the teammate passing to one goalkeeper. The opponent presses, trying to obstruct the goalkeeper from distributing the ball. The goalkeeper should decide which option is the best: the pass to the outfield teammate or the long pass over the players to the other goalkeeper. If a goalkeeper receives the ball after a long pass from the other goalkeeper, he should always play the next pass to the outfield teammate.

Advice (1) Move on tips of toes and with small steps. (2) Calculate the ball speed. (3) Keep calm. (4) Work on both feet.

Coaching Points

(1) Get in the line of the ball. (2) Keep your torso steady.
(3) Choose what is the best option and how many touches you are going to make.
(4) Decide if you are going to make a short or long pass.
(5) Good first touch. (6) Good distribution.

Assistant presses: GK decides whether to pass to red outfield teammate or other GK

Goalkeeper Training Methodology

CHAPTER 14

PHYSICAL CONDITIONING

Physical conditioning is a very important success factor for a goalkeeper. A very carefully structured program must be created, which will cover the goalkeeper's needs. "Aerobic ability", "Strength", "Speed".

"Explosiveness" and "Agility" are factors which will help goalkeepers improve their level.

In this chapter we will see how technique is combined with the physical conditioning training.

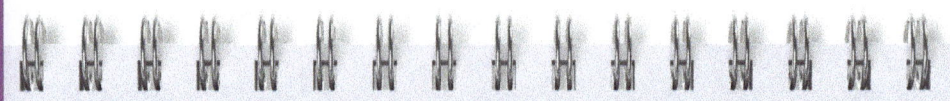

DRILL 1 AEROBIC ABILITY: FORWARD SPEED (LEVEL 1)

Description The goalkeeper stands in the middle of a 5 x 5 meter square. There is a ball in each corner and another one in the center as shown.

The goalkeeper starts in the center and jogs to touch one of the balls, then turns and returns to touch the center ball. He repeats this to touch all the balls in all the corners. He works in both directions.

Coaching Points

1. Torso remains steady.
2. Small steps.
3. Right placements of the center of gravity when changing direction.

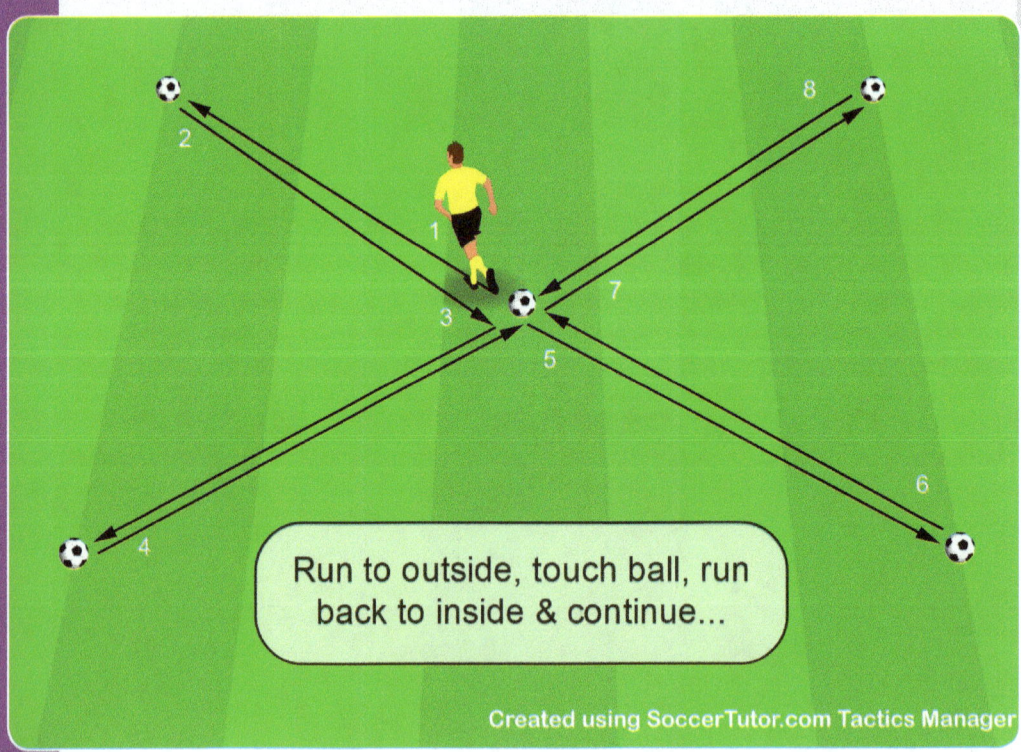

Run to outside, touch ball, run back to inside & continue...

DRILL 2   AEROBIC ABILITY: FRONT-BACK SPEED (LEVEL 2)

Description This is the same as the previous practice but now each time the goalkeeper returns to the center after touching a ball, he jogs backwards.

Coaching Points

The same as the previous drill.

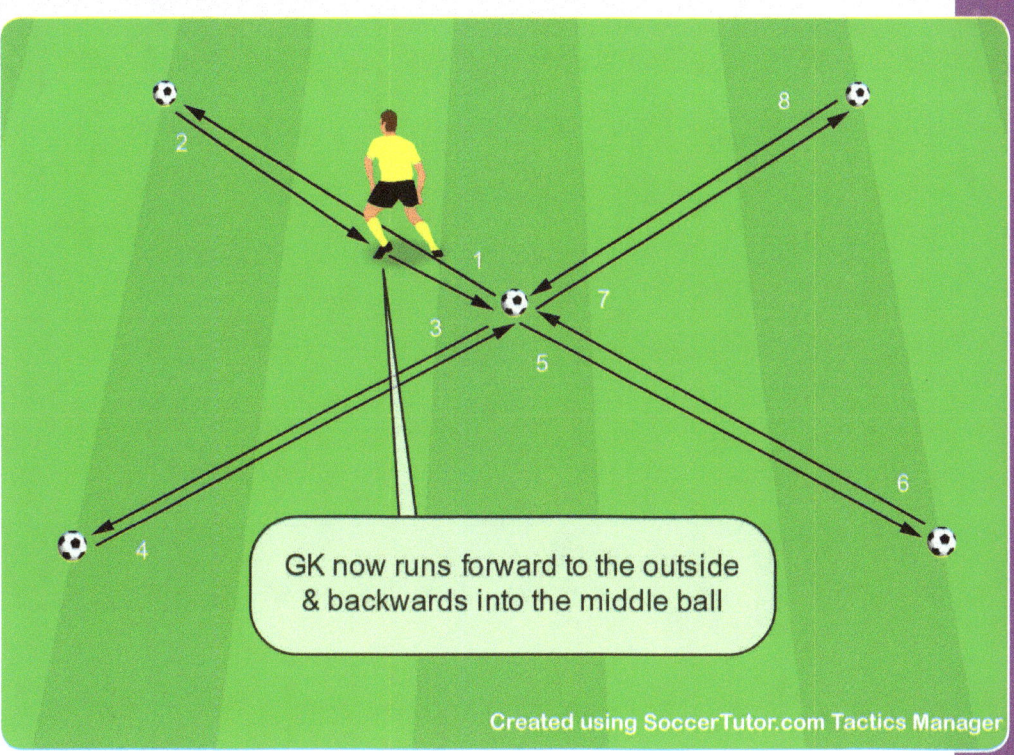

GK now runs forward to the outside & backwards into the middle ball

DRILL 3   AEROBIC ABILITY: SIDE-STEP SPEED (LEVEL 1)

Description This is the same as the previous practice but now the goalkeeper uses side-steps throughout.

Coaching Points

The same as the previous drill.

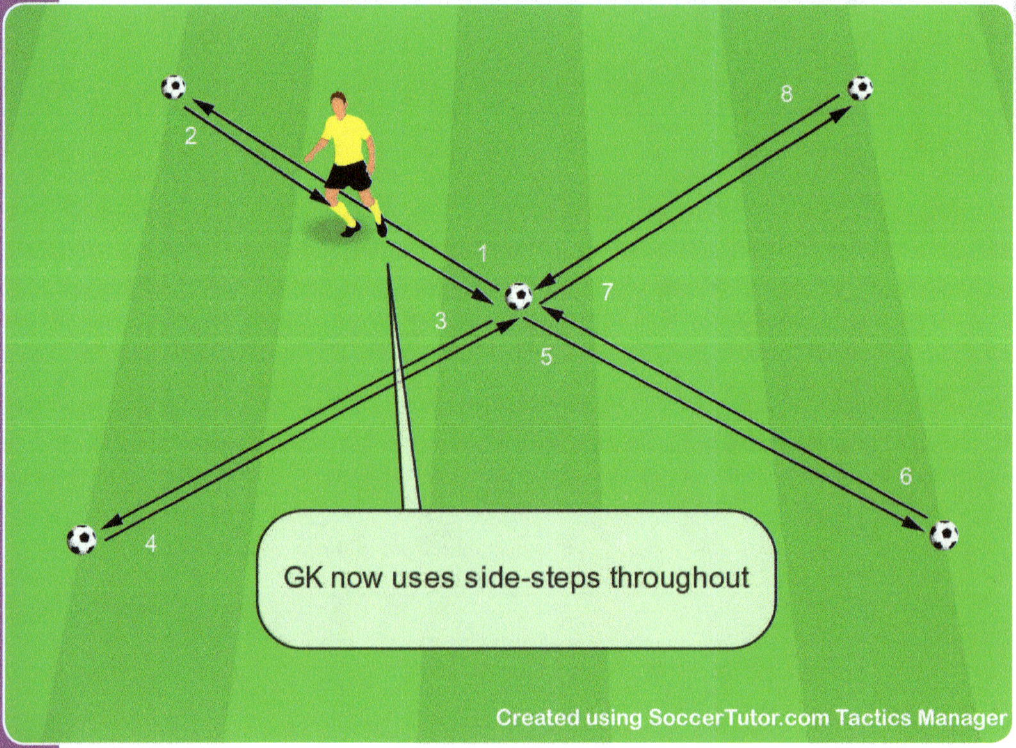

GK now uses side-steps throughout

DRILL 4 — SPEED-PICK THE BALL (LEVEL 1)

Description The goalkeeper stands in a 5 x 5 meter square. The assistant is a few meters away, in front of the goalkeeper with a ball in hands.

The assistant serves the balls to different spots within the square.

The goalkeeper runs as fast as possible, in order to catch the ball before it touches the ground for the second time.

Advice The goalkeeper can fall/dive to catch the ball.

Coaching Points

1. Torso remains steady.
2. Small steps.

Catch the ball before it bounces for a 2nd time

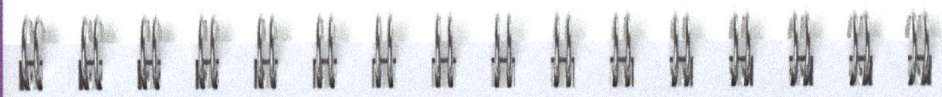

DRILL 5 RECOVERY STRENGTH AND SPEED (LEVEL 2)

Description The goalkeeper starts by lying down in a wide a side-on position. The assistant is on the other side and has ball in his hands and at his feet.

The assistant passes or throws the balls towards the side of the goal.

The goalkeeper stands up and runs to the ball to try and catch it or parry/punch it away before it crosses the goal-line.

Coaching Points

1. Quick lift from the ground.
2. Torso remains steady.
3. Small steps.

DRILL 6 — AEROBIC ABILITY AND STRENGTH: RECOVER FROM FACE DOWN WITH LEAP UP - (LEVEL 2)

Description The goalkeeper is lying on the ground (image 1). The assistant is 2 meters away with a ball in his hands. The assistant serves high balls. The goalkeeper must stand up very quickly (image 2), jump high and catch the ball (image 3). He then returns to his initial position (image 4) and repeats the same. The goalkeeper makes many repetitions.

Advice The number of repetitions depend on the age of the goalkeeper and his level. The goalkeeper starts at the voice command of the assistant. The goalkeeper can work at all possible starting positions (face down, side-on, kneeling etc.).

Coaching Points
1. Quick lift up.
2. Stand well on both feet before the leap.
3. Catch the ball at its highest point.
4. Good "W" catch.

DRILL 7 — AEROBIC ABILITY, STRENGTH & SPEED: BACKWARD MOVEMENT & SAVE FROM SITTING POSITION (LEVEL 2)

Description The goalkeeper is in a sitting position with his back to goal (image 1). The assistant is 2meters away from the goalkeeper with a ball in his hands. The assistant serves high balls trying to lob the goalkeeper.

The goalkeeper stands up very quickly, make quick steps backwards (image 2) and catch the ball at its highest point (image 3). The goalkeeper then repeats (image 4).

Advice 1 The number of repetitions depend on the age of the goalkeeper and his level. The goalkeeper starts at the voice command of the assistant.

Advice 2 The goalkeeper works from all angles of the area. The goalkeeper can work at all possible starting positions (sitting, side-on, kneeling etc.).

Coaching Points
1. Quick lift up.
2. Stand well on both feet before the leap.
3. Catch the ball at its highest point.
4. Good "W" catch.

drill 7

2

3

4

Goalkeeper Training Methodology

DRILL 8 — AEROBIC ABILITY: CONTINUOUS SAVES (LEVEL 2)

Description The goalkeeper is by the post in a ready position. There are 8-12 balls as shown. The assistant passes or shoots all the balls in turn, without giving too much recovery time to the goalkeeper.

The goalkeeper must react to all the balls with the right decisions e.g. catching or parrying. The recoveries must be quick and right to each separate ball.

Advice 1 Rest is a ratio of 3 to 1.

Advice 2 The time the assistant leave for the goalkeeper's recoveries is very important, so that he will keep his technique to a high level. In other words, the assistant must give time for the goalkeeper to make a save.

Coaching Points
1. Quick feet.
2. Good recoveries from the ground.
3. Take the straight line of each ball separately.

Assistant shoots all balls and GK must react quickly to each one

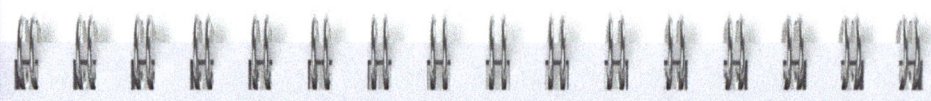

DRILL 9 — AEROBIC ABILITY: CONTINUOUS SAVES SWITCHING FROM LEFT TO RIGHT (LEVEL 2)

Description The goalkeeper starts by one post in a ready position. There are two assistants in the positions shown, one left and one right.

The first assistant has balls at his feet and passes toward one side of the goal. The second assistant then throws a ball out of his hands to the other side.

The assistants take turns, allowing the goalkeeper time to react to each ball separately.

The goalkeeper must move left and right, reacting to each ball that the assistants serve him.

Advice Repeat (e.g. 6-8 times) relevant to the age and level of the goalkeeper.

Coaching Points

1. Quick feet.
2. Good recoveries from the ground.

Assistant on left kicks the ball & assistant on right throws ball

DRILL 10   AEROBIC ABILITY: CONTINUOUS STRAIGHT SAVES (LEVEL 2)

Description The goalkeeper starts in a ready position. An assistant is 2 meters away with a ball at his feet. The assistant passes the balls to one side of the goalkeeper, forcing him to make small steps to catch the ball. This is repeated 3 or 4 times as they move along an approximate distance of 10 meters. The same is then repeated in the opposite direction. Each time the goalkeeper catches the ball, he returns it to the assistant by rolling it to his feet.

Advice 1 You can do the same practice with medium or high balls. Rest at a ratio of 3 to 1.

Advice 2 The goalkeeper must always catch the ball. The time that the assistant will leave to the goalkeeper for his recoveries is very important, so that he will keep his technique at a high level. In other words, the assistant must give the goalkeeper time to make each save.

Repeat for all balls

Created using SoccerTutor.com Tactics Manager

PARAMETERS OF PHYSICAL CONDITION ON THE INDIVIDUAL MATURITY AGE CATEGORIES

Physical conditioning is one parameter of the education and development of a goalkeeper. It is a key aspect and has to work in full collaboration with the other parameters to produce high performance and fit in with the basic training goal... the game!

Physical conditioning of goalkeepers is continuously evolving and is developed according to the age of the child.

From the moment of birth, a child trains its physical condition in an indirect way. Through the game a young child trains in a direct way and the results help the kinetic and biological development.

The first form of drill begins to take even bigger value as children get older.

If we could categorize based on age, training and physical conditioning in a game, we would categorize the development of the child as follows:

1) Age 0-4: Physical Conditioning Goal: The kinetic evolvement, through its biological development and the execution of many forms of compound drills. Meaning the Game!

2) Age 4-6: Physical Conditioning Goal: The execution of the game through the procedure of the child's socializing. The beginning of the team game and the understanding of roles and rules within the team.

3) Age 7-8: Physical Conditioning Goal: Elements like balance and the general coordination begin to complete the procedure of "I simply have fun by playing".

4) Age 9-10: Physical Conditioning Goal: The coordination starts to include bigger specialization, the balance is renamed to proprioception with the according adjustments, while the child biologically transforms all these forms of training (anaerobic, agalactic, glycolytic, oxido-glycolytic) to an aerobic form of drill. Strength is not yet valued as a physical parameter goal, not because it doesn't exist, but because it is not always part of the drills.

5) Age 11-12: Physical Conditioning Goal: In this last stage before the "harmonic revolution" of the body, we have an increase in ability to absorb new coordination moves, of proprioception and of technical demands from the game. We begin power training through learning to control the body and cope with physical contact from opponents. High aerobic ability and beginning of developing the aerobic system.

6) Age 13-14: Physical Conditioning Goal: It's the "poor in learning" but "rich in development" age. We have an increase in muscle tissue, of the body frame and of the harmonic revolution of the body, in a biologically critical period. The accuracy of the coordination is lost along with a part of proprioception and of calmness. Weakness of focus characterizes the child. Its aerobic system is rapidly matured. Production of lactic acid begins to be countable and gets value in the training procedure. Strength is improved through the use of the body, in gradually increasing forces and directions, with or without a teammate or an opponent.

7) Age 15-16: Physical Conditioning Goal: Activating of the child's energy systems. Introduction to the regular speed training, with a clearly more mature aerobic system. Application of all the kinds of cardio respiratory training, with a gradual increase of stimulations. Use of external force resistance, with a parallel increase programming, as to the variety of the drills and of the escalation of the weights.

8) Age 17-18: Physical Conditioning Goal: We have the stage of perfecting the parameters of physical conditioning. There is total maturity of the biological systems, therefore an ability for regular high tense training in all the special (or not) forms. If there has been a gradual training of their energy systems in the past, we have set the basis for a high level player.

The above confirm that the training of the developing ages is not a non-programmed and randomly structured procedure, but a strike to the GOAL of the child's energy systems, with organization, knowledge patience and LOVE!

Vaggelis Bekas
Teacher of Physical Education specialized on football

FREE TRIAL

Football Coaching Specialists Since 2001

TACTICS MANAGER
Create your own Practices, Tactics & Plan Sessions!

 www.SoccerTutor.com/TacticsManager
info@soccertutor.com

 PC   Mac   iPad   Tablet   Web

www.ingramcontent.com/pod-product-compliance
Lightning Source LLC
Chambersburg PA
CBHW061129010526
44117CB00023B/2994